TEACHING OVERWEIGHT STUDENTS IN PHYSICAL EDUCATION

COMPREHENSIVE
STRATEGIES FOR INCLUSION

BY WEIDONG LI

Routledge
Taylor & Francis Group

NEW YORK AND LONDON

First published 2017
by Routledge
711 Third Avenue, New York, NY 10017

and by Routledge
2 Park Square, Milton Park, Abingdon, Oxon, OX14 4RN

Routledge is an imprint of the Taylor & Francis Group, an informa business

© 2017 Taylor & Francis

Library of Congress Cataloging in Publication Data
A catalog record for this book has been requested

ISBN: 978-1-138-84134-5 (hbk)
ISBN: 978-1-138-84135-2 (pbk)
ISBN: 978-1-315-73200-8 (ebk)

Typeset in Minion and Scala Sans
by Apex CoVantage, LLC

To my dad, mom, wife, son, daughter, and brother for their love and support throughout my life journey.

CONTENTS

The percentage of children and adolescents who are overweight or obese in the United States has dramatically increased over the past two decades. Overweight or obese children and adolescents suffer not only from a number of obesity-related cardiovascular and heart diseases, but also from serious psychosocial damage as a result of weight stigmatization. In general, overweight or obese children and adolescents have lower physical ability, sport skills, and fitness than their normal-weight peers. Additionally, it is a common stereotype that overweight or obese children and adolescents possess undesirable characteristics such as being lazy and unmotivated, less intelligent, less attractive, or less athletic (Puhl & Latner, 2007; Zeller, Reiter-Purtill, & Ramey, 2008). As a result of these pervasive stereotypical beliefs, many overweight or obese students are commonly teased or even excluded from engaging in physical education (Fox & Edmunds, 2000; Li & Rukavina, 2012b; Trout & Graber, 2009). Research has demonstrated that weight-related teasing is related to serious psychological and emotional damage in children (Li & Rukavina, 2012b; Storch et al., 2007) and can lead overweight or obese students to distance themselves from participating in physical activity (Faith, Leone, Ayers, Heo, & Pietrobelli, 2002) or be unsatisfied with their physical education lessons (Kamtsios & Digelidis, 2008). Moreover, overweight or obese individuals can internalize these negative stereotypical beliefs, and then use maladaptive behaviors to cope with weight-related teasing—such as avoiding physical activity, binge eating, or watching television—and consequently experience further weight gain (Rukavina & Li, 2008).

The situation of overweight or obese students with regard to their low physical ability, skills, and fitness; serious obesity-related health implications; being teased and excluded from physical education by their peers; and psychosocial and emotional suffering as a result of weight stigma has presented an unprecedented challenge for teachers to include these students in physical education activities. The Standards for Initial Programs in Physical Education Teacher Education published by the National Association for Sport and Physical Education ([NASPE], 2001) indicates that physical education teachers should provide individualized instruction for diverse learners and foster positive learning environments to maximize individual student learning. However, previous research has demonstrated that physical education teachers and student teachers are negatively biased toward overweight or obese individuals (Greenleaf & Weiller, 2005; O'Brien, Hunter, & Banks, 2007). Physical education teachers often lack the knowledge and skills needed to include overweight or obese students through the creation of inclusive and safe learning climates and providing differentiated instruction in terms of their unique characteristics (Li, Rukavina, Sutherland, Shen, & Kim, 2012).

This book provides a conceptual map for successfully including overweight or obese students and offers physical education teachers practical strategies for creating inclusive and safe climates, and designing differentiated instructions to maximize overweight or obese students' engagement and learning in physical education. This book will also benefit overweight or obese students' parents by providing strategies for educating their children in how to cope with stigma and weight-related teasing. During the focus group interviews for checking the accuracy of our interpretations of the data, parents showed great appreciation for the coping strategies generated from this research project. Parents commented that they learned many good coping strategies by going through the list.

This book is based on my 10-year research in this area. It consists of five chapters. Chapter 1 discusses the obesity trend, health-related and psychosocial consequences of obesity, causes of obesity, and how to prevent obesity from an energy balance approach. Chapter 2 focuses on the introduction of weight stigma and bias, how overweight or obese students are teased in physical education (Li & Rukavina, 2012b), and the negative effects of weight-related teasing on overweight or obese students' overall well-being. Chapter 3 introduces coping and discusses how overweight or obese students cope with weight-related teasing, and what teachers can do to deal with weight-related teasing in physical education (Li, Rukavina, & Wright, 2012). Chapter 4 presents the conceptual model: Social Ecological Constraint Model (Li & Rukavina, 2012a). In this model, as reflected in Figure 4.1, the teacher is an agent of change who will be made aware of and manipulate a variety of factors from five different levels for effective inclusion of overweight students in physical education: individual overweight students, instructional settings, school/family, community, and society. Finally, Chapter 5 provides instructors with detailed strategies guided by the conceptual model that can be implemented into their inclusive physical education classes.

This book is conceptually based, comprehensive, evidence based, and timely, which will help physical education teachers create inclusive and safe climates, and design a variety of lessons to motivate and engage overweight or obese students in physical education.

References

Faith, M. S., Leone, M. A., Ayers, T. S., Heo, M., & Pietrobelli, A. (2002). Weight criticism during physical activity, coping skills, and reported physical activity in children. *Pediatrics, 110*, e23.

Fox, K. R., & Edmunds, L. D. (2000). Understanding the world of the "fat kid": Schools help provide a better experience? *Reclaiming Child Youth: Journal of Emotion Behavior Problems, 9*, 177–181.

Greenleaf, C., & Weiller, K. (2005). Perceptions of youth obesity among physical educators. *Social Psychology of Education, 8*, 407–423.

Kamtsios, S., & Digelidis, N. (2008). Physical activity levels, exercise attitudes, self-perceptions and BMI type of 11 to 12 year old children. *Journal of Child Health Care, 12*(3), 232–240.

Li, W., & Rukavina, P. (2012a). Including overweight or obese students in physical education: A social ecological constraint model. *Research Quarterly for Exercise and Sport, 83*(9), 570–578.

Li, W., & Rukavina, P. (2012b). The nature, occurring contexts, and psychological implications of weight-related teasing in urban physical education programs. *Research Quarterly for Exercise and Sport, 83*, 308–317.

Li, W., Rukavina, P., Sutherland, S., Shen, B., & Kim, I. (2012). Physical education in the eyes of overweight or obese adolescents' parents. *Journal of Sport Behavior, 35*, 204–222.

Li, W., Rukavina, P., & Wright, P. M. (2012). Coping against weight-related teasing among overweight or obese adolescents in urban physical education. *Journal of Teaching in Physical Education, 31*, 182–199.

National Association for Sport and Physical Education [NASPE]. (2001). *National standards for beginning physical education teachers.* Reston, VA: Author.

O'Brien, K. S., Hunter, J. A., & Banks, M. (2007). Implicit anti-fat bias in physical educators: Physical attributes, ideology, and socialization. *International Journal of Obesity, 31*, 308–314.

Puhl, R. M., & Latner, J. (2007). Stigma, obesity, and the health of the nation's children. *Psychological Bulletin, 133*(4), 557–580.

Rukavina, P., & Li, W. (2008). School physical activity interventions: Do not forget about obesity bias. *Obesity Reviews, 9*, 67–75.

Storch, E. A., Milsom, V. A., DeBraganza, N., Lewin, A. B., Geffken, G. R., & Silverstein, J. H. (2007). Peer victimization, psychosocial adjustment, and physical activity in overweight and at-risk-for-overweight youth. *Journal of Pediatric Psychology, 32*, 80–89.

Trout, J., & Graber, K. C. (2009). Perceptions of overweight students concerning their experience in physical education. *Journal of Teaching in Physical Education, 28*, 272–292.

Zeller, M. H., Reiter-Purtill, J., & Ramey, C. (2008). Negative peer perceptions of obese children in the classroom environment. *Obesity, 16*(4), 755–762.

Acknowledgments

I would like to thank American Alliance for Health, Physical Education, Recreation, and Dance (currently known as the Society of Health and Physical Educators: SHAPE of America) Research Consortium grant programs for their funding of research projects. The data from these research projects has made this manuscript possible.

I am especially thankful for the study participants for sharing their experiences with me. The experience has affected not only my professional life but also my personal life.

I owe a great deal of gratitude to the editors from Taylor & Francis, Georgette Enriquez and Gail Fay, who provided expert guidance.

1

OBESITY AND OBESITY-RELATED CONSEQUENCES

This chapter introduces the definition of obesity and prevalence of obesity, discusses the etiology of obesity, and describes physical, psychosocial, emotional, and behavioral consequences of obesity. The final section presents the benefits of physical activity. The information provided in this chapter will help physical education teachers understand the complexity of obesity, and equip them with knowledge and skills to raise awareness about obesity among their students. Instructors will be able to promote physical education in their school as well as obtain better resources and support from their administrators and colleagues.

Definition of Obesity

Obesity refers to a condition in which a person has excessive accumulation and storage of body fat (*Merriam Webster's Online*

Dictionary). The most commonly used measure of body fat is body mass index (BMI), which is calculated by a formula—dividing squared body height in meters by body weight in kilograms. According to the Centers for Disease Control and Prevention [CDC] (2015a), adults can be classified as being underweight, normal weight, overweight, or obese based on their BMI. A high BMI generally means high body fat.

- Underweight: BMI less than 18.5
- Normal or healthy weight: BMI from 18.5 to 24.9
- Overweight: BMI from 25.0 to 29.9
- Obese: BMI of 30.0 or higher

Children and adolescents' BMI is compared to growth charts that are age and gender specific. Based on the growth charts, a child can be classified as underweight, normal or healthy weight, overweight, or obese (CDC, 2015a). A high percentile generally indicates high fat.

- Underweight: BMI-for-age less than 5th percentile
- Normal or healthy weight: BMI-for-age from 5th percentile to less than 85th percentile
- Overweight: BMI-for-age from 85th percentile to less than 95th percentile
- Obese: BMI-for-age of 95th percentile or higher

BMI is not a golden measurement of body fat, and there are many issues related to BMI such as inaccuracy. However, BMI screening is low cost and very practical as it can be administered to a large group of students in a short period of time in physical education classes. Many U.S. states have enacted legislation to require BMI screening in public schools: Arkansas, Florida, Maine, Massachusetts, Nevada, New Jersey, New

York, Pennsylvania, Tennessee, and West Virginia. Many researchers and practitioners view BMI screening in public schools as one policy approach to addressing the problem of childhood obesity. However, this policy has created a lot of controversies. According to Ikeda, Crawford, and Woodward-Lopez (2006), BMI screening has many pros and cons. The pros are:

- It raises parental awareness of their child's weight status after reviewing their child's BMI screening results.
- It encourages parents to assess and potentially change the diet and activity patterns of their children as a means to treat or prevent overweight and obesity.
- This type of mandatory measurement of BMI allows for monitoring childhood obesity trends.
- It provides important information for the development and implementation of successful strategies and interventions aimed at obesity treatment and prevention.

The cons for conducting BMI screening at schools are:

- Children are labeled. This can increase weight-related teasing toward overweight or obese students.
- Children can potentially develop eating disorder symptoms as a result of becoming thin and slim (Cogan, Smith, & Maine, 2008; Ikeda et al., 2006).

Given the potential negative unintended consequences of BMI screening, physical education teachers should take precautions before conducting BMI screening at their schools, including checking out their own state legislation and school district policies, gaining approval and support from school principals, collaborating with school counselors and nurses, and surveying parents to get their perspectives on BMI screening.

The Prevalence of Obesity in the United States

Since 1985, the obesity rate has increased dramatically in the United States. Even today, obesity is still widespread and at the forefront of the public health crisis in the United States (Ogden et al., 2014; Ogden et al., 2015). It is estimated that 69% of adults are overweight or obese, and 35% of adults are obese. Among children and adolescents, over 30% are overweight or obese. Seventeen percent of children and adolescents are obese (Ogden et al., 2015).

Many racial-ethnic and geographic disparities exist in the rates of overweight or obesity among adults and children (Ogden et al., 2014). In general, African-American and Hispanic women have higher rates of overweight or obesity than Caucasian women. Hispanic men have higher rates of overweight or obesity than African-American and Caucasian men. The overweight and obesity rates are higher in the South and Midwest regions (Gregg et al., 2009; Ogden et al., 2014; Sherry et al., 2010). Among children, African-American and Hispanic children tend to have higher rates of overweight or obesity than Caucasian children (Freedman et al., 2006; Ogden et al., 2014). The rates of overweight or obesity tend to be higher among children from families with a lower social economic class (Ogden et al., 2014; Wang & Zhang, 2006) and living in the Southern region of the United States (Singh et al., 2008).

Etiology of Obesity

The etiology of obesity is complicated. Numerous factors can contribute to obesity, including individual lifestyle behaviors, genetic makeups, medical conditions, prescription medication side effects, social and cultural norms, and environments

(Anderson & Butcher, 2006). Other factors contributing to obesity include the following:

- Medical conditions such as polycystic ovary syndrome can cause obesity.
- Some prescription drugs such as steroids and antidepressants can lead to obesity.
- Environmental factors: Physical activity and food environments can also contribute to obesity (Sallis & Glanz, 2009). An overabundance of fast food choices (high fat and junk food), a dangerous neighborhood, lack of access to physical activity in the community, and an increasing availability of television and video games all can contribute to obesity.
- Social and cultural factors: Poor, less educated Americans are more likely to be overweight or obese than those who are wealthy and more educated. Individuals from a low socioeconomic class may not have enough money to purchase healthy foods to eat. Less educated Americans may not receive adequate education on how to cook healthy meals. African-Americans and Hispanic-Americans are more likely to accept a larger body size than others (Haytko, Parker, Motley, & Torres, 2014).
- Psychological factors: Individuals are likely to gain weight from excess calories in response to emotional stress such as loneliness, pain, rejection, anxiety, or anger (Gundersen, Mahatmya, Garasky, & Lohman, 2011).
- Genetics: Obesity runs in families. Children with one obese parent or two parents who are overweight or obese are more likely to become overweight or obese than those whose parents have normal weight (Choquet & Meyre, 2011).
- Individuals' lifestyle behaviors: An individual who does not get enough sleep or sleeps too much can gain an appetite as a result of changes in hormones (Knutson, 2012). One

can crave foods high in calories and carbohydrates. Consequently, he or she can gain body weight. An individual who lives a sedentary lifestyle is more likely to gain body weight as he or she takes in more calories than he or she burns. Eating an unhealthy diet high in calories can also contribute to an increase in a person's body weight.

Among all these factors, individual lifestyle behaviors such as lack of physical activity and unhealthy diet are the leading causes of overweight and obesity. Therefore, lifestyle interventions play a critical role in decreasing the overweight and obesity rates in the United States.

Consequences of Obesity

Childhood obesity is associated with serious *physiological consequences* (Daniels, 2009; Ebbeling et al., 2002; Franks et al., 2010; Olshansky et al., 2005; Papoutsakis et al., 2013; Tsiros et al., 2009; Visness et al., 2009), *psychosocial consequences* (Anderson et al., 2007; BeLue et al., 2009; Boutelle et al., 2010; Carey et al., 2015; Haines & Neumark-Sztainer, 2006; Li & Rukavina, 2012; Neumark-Sztainer et al., 2002; Puhl & Latner, 2007; Shore et al., 2008), and *economic consequences* (Cawley, 2010; Cawley & Meyerhoefer, 2012; Finkelstein, Ruhm, & Kosa, 2005). This is very alarming since many of these consequences will manifest later in life, and children who are overweight or obese are more likely to become more overweight or obese as adults (Freedman et al., 2005). The physiological consequences of childhood obesity follow:

- Children who are overweight or obese are at a high risk of experiencing a potential decline in life expectancy. This generation of children may have a shorter longevity than their parents due to a high prevalence of obesity (Olshansky et al., 2005).

- Children who are overweight or obese are at a high risk of having diabetes, atherosclerosis, dyslipidemia (e.g., high blood triglycerides, high cholesterol), high blood pressure, metabolic syndrome, liver disease, sleep apnea, disordered breathing, and orthopedic complications (Daniels, 2009).

- Children who are overweight or obese are at a high risk of developing gall bladder disease (Ebbeling et al., 2002), asthma (Papoutsakis et al., 2013), and allergies (Visness et al., 2009).

- Children who are overweight or obese are associated with poor health-related life quality (Tsiros et al., 2009) and are more likely to have premature death later in life (Franks et al., 2010).

- Children who are overweight or obese are more likely to have bone and joint disorders (Marder & Chang, 2005).

The psychosocial consequences of childhood obesity follow:

- Children who are overweight or obese are more likely to develop depressive symptoms (Boutelle et al., 2010) and anxiety symptoms (Anderson et al., 2007).

- Children who are overweight or obese are more likely to display poor body image (Averett & Korenman, 1999), have low self-esteem (McClure et al., 2010), feel worthless and inferior to their peers (BeLue et al., 2009), and show body dissatisfaction (Neumark-Sztainer et al., 2002).

- Children who are overweight or obese are more likely to experience peer victimization and be stigmatized and teased (Eisenberg et al., 2003; Li & Rukavina, 2012; Puhl & Latner, 2007).

- Children who are overweight or obese are more likely to display disordered eating and unhealthy weight-control behaviors (Haines & Neumark-Sztainer, 2006; Neumark-Sztainer et al., 2002).
- Children who are overweight or obese are more likely to have more school absences and lower academic performance (Carey et al., 2015; Shore et al., 2008).
- Children who are overweight or obese are more likely to have mental health disorders (Marder & Chang, 2005).

In addition to serious physiological and psychosocial consequences, obesity has economic costs that can affect all of us. Obesity is costly both to the individual and to society. The annual health care expenditures for obesity-related illness are estimated at $190.2 billion in the United States (Cawley & Meyerhoefer, 2012). Obesity costs billions of dollars to businesses in the United States due to paid sick leave, life insurance, disability, lost work days, restricted activity days, bed days, and physician visits. The aggregate annual obesity-related medical costs contribute to 5% and 7% of total annual health care expenditures (Finkelstein et al., 2005). The cost for children with private insurance and children enrolled in Medicaid is $11 billion and $3 billion, respectively (Marder & Chang, 2005).

Benefits of Physical Activity

The 2008 Physical Activity Guidelines Advisory Committee recommends that individuals engage in at least 60 minutes of moderate to vigorous physical activity on a daily basis to obtain health benefits (U.S. Department of Health and Human Services [USDHHS], 2008). Individuals can gain not only physical and psychosocial health benefits, but also cognitive benefits from physical activity (American College of Sports Medicine,

2009; CDC, 2015b; Haskell et al., 2007; USDHHS, 2008). Given that approximately one-third of children and adolescents are overweight or obese, it is very important to educate students on these benefits. Knowledge of benefits of physical activity has great potential to motivate students to develop and maintain a healthy and physically active lifestyle. The physical and psycho-social benefits include:

- Lower mortality from all causes
- Lower blood pressure
- Better cardio-respiratory functioning
- Lower risk of heart disease and stroke
- Lower risk of cancer, especially colon cancer and breast cancer
- Lower risk of type 2 diabetes
- Lower risk of osteoporosis and related fractures
- Better bone density
- Lower risk of falls
- Lower risk of gall bladder disease
- Better body composition
- Prevention of unhealthy weight gain
- Better quality of sleep
- Higher self-esteem
- Better mood
- Lower risk of depression and anxiety
- Improved physical fitness
- Better performance in work, leisure, and sport activities
- Better life quality
- Better blood sugar and insulin levels
- Reduced risk for chronic diseases and disabilities
- Decreased behavioral problems
- Lower risk of obesity

In addition to physical and mental health benefits, individuals can gain cognitive benefits from physical activity. Ample evidence from research supports the conclusion that physical activity is positively linked to improved cognition and better academic performance (Sibley & Etnier, 2003; Singh et al., 2012; Tomporowski et al., 2008; USDHHS, 2008). Students who are physically active have better attention spans in the classroom and obtain better cognitive functions and academic performance than those who are inactive.

Many potential mechanisms linking physical activity to achievement and cognitive ability have been proposed to explain these relations. These mechanisms can be sorted into two categories: physiological and learning/developmental mechanisms (Sibley & Etnier, 2003). The physiological mechanisms include increased cerebral blood flow and neural connections in brain areas, structural changes in the central nervous system, stimulation of the prefrontal cortex used in learning and problem-solving, and alterations in arousal levels. Increased physical activity during school may alter arousal level and reduce boredom, which can increase students' attention span and concentration. In a review on physical activity and academic performance, Almond and McGeorge (1998) reported that exercise leads to direct physical changes such as hormone levels, increased cerebral blood flow during aerobic exercises, and acceleration of psychomotor skills. Shephard (1997) found that the enhanced arousal levels and boredom reduction that occur with physical activity resulted in more attention to instruction in the classroom. Those physiological changes associated with physical activity may explain the improved achievement and academic ability. According to the learning/developmental mechanisms, children gain learning experience through physical activity, and these experience not only facilitate but may be a necessity for developing appropriate cognitive ability (Sibley & Etnier, 2003). For example, by actively participating in physical activity, children can achieve better academic attitudes, enhanced self-esteem, and better self-control ability as a result of an increase of motor skills, stronger muscle, and better appearance. Those improvements in attitude, self-esteem, and self-control may be the reason for the enhanced academic performance (Bluechardt, Wiener, & Shephard, 1995; Shephard, 1997).

Summary

The obesity rate has tripled since 1980. There are numerous factors that can cause childhood obesity. The etiology of obesity is complicated. Obesity has not only physiological and psychosocial consequences but also economic consequences. For more resources and information, physical education teachers can visit the Centers for Disease Control and Prevention's website at http://www.cdc.gov/obesity/childhood/causes.html.

Children and adolescents can gain physical, mental, and cognitive benefits from physical activity. The information provided herein will help physical education teachers develop an education module to raise awareness among their students about obesity and its consequences and motivate students to develop and maintain a healthy, physically active lifestyle. It also will help instructors promote physical education in their school and obtain resources and support from school administrators and colleagues to create an inclusive physical activity–friendly environment, where all students can have numerous opportunities to be physically active.

References

Almond, L., & McGeorge, S. (1998). Physical activity and academic performance. *The British Journal of Physical Education, 29*, 8–11.

American College of Sports Medicine. (2009). Physical activity and public health: Updated recommendation for adults from the American College of Sports Medicine and the American Heart Association. *Medicine and Science in Sports and Exercise, 39*(8), 1423–1434.

Anderson, P. M., & Butcher, K. F. (2006). Childhood obesity: Trends and potential causes. *The Future of Children, 16*(1), 19–45.

Anderson, S. E., Cohen, P., Naumova, E. N., Jacques, P. F., & Must, A. (2007). Adolescent obesity and risk for subsequent major depressive disorder and anxiety disorder: Prospective evidence. *Psychosomatic Medicine, 69*(8), 740–747.

Averett, S., & Korenman, S. (1999). Black-white differences in social and economic consequences of obesity. *International Journal of Obesity, 23,* 166–173.

BeLue, R., Francis, L. A., & Colaco, B. (2009). Mental health problems and overweight in a nationally representative sample of adolescents: Effects of race and ethnicity. *Pediatrics, 123*(2), 697–702.

Bluechardt, M., Wiener, J., & Shephard, R. J. (1995). Exercise programs in the treatment of children with learning disabilities. *Sports Medicine, 19,* 55–72.

Boutelle, K. N., Hannan, P., Fulkerson, J. A., Crow, S. J., & Stice, E. (2010). Obesity as a prospective predictor of depression in adolescent females. *Health Psychology, 29*(3), 293–298.

Carey, F. R., Singh, G. K., Brown, H. S., & Wilkinson, A. V. (2015). Educational outcomes associated with childhood obesity in the United States: Cross-sectional results from the 2011–2012 National Survey of Children's Health. *International Journal of Behavioral Nutrition and Physical Activity, 12*(Supplement 1), S3.

Cawley, J. (2010). The economics of childhood obesity. *Health Affairs (Millwood), 29*(3), 364–371.

Cawley, J., & Meyerhoefer, C. (2012). The medical care costs of obesity: An instrumental variables approach. *Journal of Health Economy, 31*(1), 219–230.

Centers for Disease Control and Prevention. (2015a). *Assessing your weight.* Available at: http://www.cdc.gov/healthyweight/assessing/index.html

Centers for Disease Control and Prevention. (2015b). *Physical activity and health.* Available at: http://www.cdc.gov/physicalactivity/basics/pa-health/

Choquet, H., & Meyre, D. (2011). Genetics of obesity: What have we learned? *Current Genomics, 12*(3), 169–179.

Cogan, J. C., Smith, J. P., & Maine, M. D. (2008). The risks of a quick fix: A case against mandatory body mass index reporting laws. *Eating Disorder, 16*(1), 2–13.

Daniels, S. R. (2009). Complications of obesity in children and adolescents. *International Journal of Obesity, 33*(Supplement 1), S60–S65.

Ebbeling, C. B., Pawlak, D. B., & Ludwig, D. S. (2002). Childhood obesity: Public-health crisis, common sense cure. *Lancet, 360*(9331), 473–482.

Eisenberg, M. E., Neumark-Sztainer, D., & Story, M. (2003). Associations of weight-based teasing and emotional well-being among adolescents. *Archives of Pediatric and Adolescent Medicine, 157*(8), 733–738.

Finkelstein, E. A., Ruhm, C. J., & Kosa, K. M. (2005). Economic causes and consequences of obesity. *Annual Review of Public Health, 26*, 239–257.

Franks, P. W., Hanson, R. L., Knowler, W. C., Sievers, M. L., Bennett, P. H., & Looker, H. C. (2010). Childhood obesity, other cardiovascular risk factors, and premature death. *New England Journal of Medicine, 362*(6), 485–493.

Freedman, D. S., Khan, L. K., Serdula, M. K., Dietz, W. H., Srinivasan, S. R., & Berenson, G. S. (2005). The relation of childhood BMI to adult adiposity: The Bogalusa heart study. *Pediatrics, 115*(1), 22–27.

Freedman, D. S., Khan, L. K., Serdula, M. K., Ogden, C. L., & Dietz, W. H. (2006). Racial and ethnic differences in secular trends for childhood BMI, weight, and height. *Obesity, 14*(2), 301–308.

Gregg, E. W., Kirtland, K. A., Cadwell, B. L., Rios Burrows, N., Barker, L. E., Thompson, T. J., Geiss, L., & Pan, L. (2009). Estimated county-level prevalence of diabetes and obesity—United States, 2007. *Morbidity and Mortality Weekly Report, 58*(45), 1259–1263.

Gundersen, C., Mahatmya, D., Garasky, S., & Lohman, B. (2011). Linking psychosocial stressors and childhood obesity. *Obesity Reviews, 12*(5), e54–e63.

Haines, J., & Neumark-Sztainer, D. (2006). Prevention of obesity and eating disorders: A consideration of shared risk factors. *Health Education Research, 21*(6), 770–782.

Haskell, W. L., Lee, I. M., Pate, R. R., Powell, K. E., Blair, S. N., Franklin, B. A., Macera, C. A., Heath, G. W., Thompson, P. D., & Bauman, A. (2007). Physical activity and public health: Updated recommendation for adults from the American College of Sports Medicine and the American Heart Association. *Medicine and Science in Sports and Exercise, 39*(8), 1423–1434.

Haytko, D. L., Parker, R. S., Motley, C. M., & Torres, I. M. (2014). Body image and ethnicity: A qualitative exploration. *Journal of Management and Marketing Research, 17*, 1–20.

Ikeda, J. P., Crawford, P. B., & Woodward-Lopez, G. (2006). BMI screening in schools: Helpful or harmful. *Health Education Research, 21*(6), 761–769.

Knutson, K. L. (2012). Does inadequate sleep play a role in vulnerability to obesity? *American Journal of Human Biology, 24*(3), 361–371.

Li, W., & Rukavina, P. (2012). The nature, occurring contexts, and psychological implications of weight-related teasing in urban physical education programs. *Research Quarterly for Exercise and Sport, 83*(2), 308–317.

Marder, W. D., & Chang, S. (2005). *Childhood obesity: Costs, treatment patterns, disparities in care, and prevalent medical conditions.* Thomson Medstat Research Brief. Available at: http://www.nptinternal.org/productions/chcv2/healthupdates/pdf/Cost_of_childhood_obesity.pdf

McClure, A. C., Tanski, S. E., Kingsbury, J., Gerrard, M., & Sargent, J. D. (2010). Characteristics associated with low self-esteem among U.S. adolescents. *Academic Pediatrics, 10*(4), 238–244.

Merriam Webster's Online Dictionary. (n.d.). "Obesity". Available at: http://www.merriam-webster.com/dictionary/obesity

Neumark-Sztainer, D., Story, M., Hannan, P. J., Perry, C. L., & Irving, L. M. (2002). Weight-related concerns and behaviors among overweight and non-overweight adolescents: Implications for preventing weight-related disorders. *Archives of Pediatric and Adolescent Medicine, 156*(2), 171–178.

Ogden, C. L., Carroll, M. D., Fryar, C. D., & Flegal, K. M. (2015). Prevalence of obesity among adults and youth: United States, 2011–2014. *NCHS Data Brief, 291*, 1–6.

Ogden, C. L., Carroll, M. D., Kit, B. K., & Flegal, K. M. (2014). Prevalence of childhood and adult obesity in the United States, 2011–2012. *Journal of the American Medical Association, 311*(8), 806–814.

Olshansky, S. J., Passaro, D. J., Hershow, R. C., Layden, J., Carnes, B. A., Brody, J., . . . Ludwig, D. S. (2005). A potential decline in life expectancy in the United States in the 21st century. *New England Journal of Medicine, 352*(11), 1138–1145.

Papoutsakis, C., Priftis, K. N., Drakouli, M., Prifti, S., Konstantaki, E., Chondronikola, M., Antonogeorgos, G., & Matziou, V. (2013). Childhood overweight/obesity and asthma: Is there a link? A systematic review of recent epidemiologic evidence. *Journal of the Academy of Nutrition and Dietetics, 113*(1), 77–105.

Puhl, R. M., & Latner, J. D. (2007). Stigma, obesity, and the health of the nation's children. *Psychological Bulletin, 133*(4), 557–580.

Sallis, J. F., & Glanz, K. (2009). Physical activity and food environments: Solutions to the obesity epidemic. *Milbank Quarterly, 87*(1), 123–154.

Shephard, R. J. (1997). Curricular physical activity and academic performance. *Pediatric Exercise Science, 9*, 113–126.

Sherry, B., Blanck, H. M., Galuska, D. A., Pan, L., Dietz, W. H., & Balluz, L. (2010). Vital signs: Statespecific obesity prevalence among adults—United States, 2009. *Morbidity and Mortality Weekly Report, 59*(30), 951–955.

Shore, S., Sachs, M., Lidicker, J., Brett, S., Wright, A., & Libonati, J. (2008). Decreased scholastic achievement in overweight middle school students. *Obesity, 16*, 1535–1538.

Sibley, B. A., & Etnier, J. L. (2003). The relationship between physical activity and cognition in children: A meta-analysis. *Pediatric Exercise Science, 15,* 243–256.

Singh, A., Uijtdewilligen, L., Twisk, J. W. R., van Mechelen, W., & Chinapaw, M. J. M. (2012). Physical activity and performance at school: A systematic review of the literature including a methodological quality assessment. *Archives of Pediatric and Adolescent Medicine, 166*(1), 49–55.

Singh, G. K., Kogan, M. D., & van Dyck, P. C. (2008). A multilevel analysis of state and regional disparities in childhood and adolescent obesity in the United States. *Journal of Community Health, 33*(2), 90–102.

Tomporowski, P. D., Davis, C. L., Miller, P. H., & Naglieri, J. A. (2008). Exercise and children's intelligence, cognition, and academic achievement. *Educational Psychological Review, 20,* 111–131.

Tsiros, M. D., Olds, T., Buckley, J. D., Grimshaw, P., Brennan, L., Walkley, J., Hills, A. P., Howe, P. R., & Coates, A. M. (2009). Health-related quality of life in obese children and adolescents. *International Journal of Obesity, 33*(4), 387–400.

U.S. Department of Health and Human Services. (2008). *Physical activity guidelines advisory committee report.* Washington, DC: Author.

Visness, C. M., London, S. J., Daniels, J. L., Kaufman, J. S., Yeatts, K. B., Siega-Riz, A. M., Liu, A. H., Calatroni, A., & Zeldin, D. C. (2009). Association of obesity with IgE levels and allergy symptoms in children and adolescents: Results from the National Health and Nutrition Examination Survey 2005–2006. *Journal of Allergy and Clinical Immunology, 123*(5), 1163–1169.

Wang, Y., & Zhang, Q. (2006). Are American children and adolescents of low socioeconomic status at increased risk of obesity? Changes in the association between overweight and family income between 1971 and 2002. *American Journal of Clinical Nutrition, 84,* 707–716.

2

WEIGHT STIGMA AND
OBESITY BIAS

As discussed in Chapter 1, obesity has a negative effect on students' physical health and overall well-being. Students who are overweight or obese are at a higher risk of developing diabetes, depression, or heart disease than their normal-weight peers (U.S. Department of Health and Human Services [USDHSS], 1996). Not only do overweight or obese students experience these serious obesity-related health consequences, they also suffer many social unpleasantries. Overweight and obese students are often targets of stigmatization and biases held by the general public. Students who are overweight and obese are viewed as being stupid/unsmart, bad, ugly/unattractive, lazy/unmotivated, and incompetent due to their body weight (Puhl & Brownell, 2001). Many terms have been used interchangeably to describe stigmatizing beliefs and biases that overweight or obese students experience, including weight bias, weight stigma, obesity bias, obesity stigma, weight stigmatization, and so on. Throughout this book, we use *obesity bias* for consistency.

In this chapter, obesity bias is defined, followed by discussions on obesity bias in physical education and how it affects overweight or obese students' motivation, engagement, and learning. Research on obesity bias interventions will be presented, and reactive and preventive teaching strategies will be provided for physical education teachers to cope with obesity bias. Based on the literature, it is recommended that a comprehensive school-wide and long-term approach targeting multiple sources at multiple levels be used to reduce obesity bias.

What Is Obesity Bias?

Obesity bias refers to the negative judgments that people hold against overweight or obese individuals on the basis of their stigmatized attributes (Rukavina & Li, 2008). There exist two different types of obesity bias—implicit and explicit (Puhl & Brownell, 2001). Implicit bias is defined as negative attitudes, beliefs, or behaviors toward overweight or obese individuals expressed by a person beyond his or her consciousness. Very often, individuals are unaware of their implicit bias, which operates automatically when an environmental cue is present. For example, when someone makes a comment about overweight or obese students being unmotivated, a person with an implicit bias may agree with it in silence or laugh at it. On the other hand, explicit bias refers to negative attitudes, beliefs, or behaviors that are consciously expressed toward overweight or obese students. Obesity bias can come in many different forms, including verbal comments such as ridicule, teasing, insults, mocking, joking, gossiping, rumor spreading, and name-calling, or in the form of physical confrontations such as pushing, touching, grabbing, punching, hitting, kicking, or other aggressive behaviors (Neumark-Sztainer, Story, & Faibisch, 1998; Puhl & Latner, 2007).

Children as young as 3 to 5 years old, while imitating adult behaviors, can begin to express stigmatizing beliefs and bias toward overweight or obese individuals (Cramer & Steinwert, 1998; Margulies, Floyd, & Hojnoski, 2008; Su & Santo, 2011). It has been reported that preschool children hold negative attitudes and judgments toward their obese peers (Margulies et al., 2008). This obesity bias gets stronger as children age (Klaczynski, Daniel, & Keller, 2009). A study of children aged 11–16 showed that overweight and obese girls (aged 11–16) and boys (aged 11–12) were more likely to be teased and experience relational bullying (e.g., to be socially excluded) than their normal-weight peers (Janssen, Craig, Boyce, & Pickett, 2004). Overweight or obese girls experience more weight stigmatization and bias than overweight or obese boys, and they are at a higher risk of being socially marginalized in friendships and romantic relationships (Tang-Peronard & Heitmann, 2008).

Obesity Bias in Physical Education

Obesity bias is especially relevant and widespread in school physical education. The prevalence of obesity bias in physical education occurs for different reasons. First, students' body sizes, skill levels, and abilities are on public display. In physical education, students learn how to play sports, perform exercises, and physical activities. While performing these sports and activities, students can see one another's body movements and performances. Second, overweight or obese students generally have lower skill levels and abilities in sports as compared to their normal-weight peers due to their body weight. They cannot run as fast or jump as far or high as their normal-weight peers, and perform worse in numerous sports and exercise than their normal-weight peers.

This public display of inferior skill level and ability in front of their peers can cause overweight or obese students to feel self-conscious of their body size, and thus not fully engage in sports and physical activities. For example, one overweight or obese student was self-conscious of his body when he could not do fitness activies as well as his peers, saying,

> I will be doing some push-ups and stuff like that and coach will be like you need to get up and do them. I will be doing them, but I won't be that high, then everybody turns around and looks at me. Then one time sweat got in my eye and I felt it and everybody was looking at me and all that kind of stuff.
>
> Sit-ups, I was trying to do this, but I couldn't feel my legs, and I had laid my legs down and they were like "Can't you bend your legs, tubbo?"

Student disengagement and disrespectful behaviors are prevalent in physical education programs, especially in urban settings (Cothran & Ennis, 1999; Ennis et al., 1997; Ennis et al., 1999). The negative social interactions among students in physical education can foster a negative learning environment, where overweight or obese students have little or no social support from their peers. This self-consiousness of body size and unsupportive gym environments can make overweight or obese students more vulnerable to obesity bais.

Obesity bias toward overweight or obese students has been well documented in physical education (Bauer, Yang, & Austin, 2004; Fox & Edmunds, 2000; Li & Rukavina, 2012; Trout & Graber, 2009). Li and Rukavina (2012) reported that 68% of overweight or obese adolescents experienced negative assumptions with regard to their capabilities by their peers in physical education. Overweight or obese students are perceived as having inferior social skills and being unable to make any friends.

They are perceived as having characteristics such as being lazy and unmotivated and as having a bad personality or temper. When overweight or obese students sit out of an exericse due to an injury, their peers think that they are just being lazy and do not want to do any of the exercises. Overweight or obese students are also perceived as having inferior athletic skills and abilities such as not being able to run fast, being too slow and heavy to play sports, and not being able to do many push-ups and sit-ups. For example, during fitness activities, when overweight or obese students had to run a mile on the track, their peers did not believe that they could do it and suggested that they might just sit down. However, these overweight or obese students very often proved their peers wrong by successfully completing a 1-mile run. As a result of these negative assumptions, overweight or obese students are often selected for teams last and assume a lesser role on the team where they do not need to run a lot, for example, being a goalkeeper during a soccer game.

Approximately 64% of overweight or obese students are teased or bullied by their peers in physical education classes (Li & Rukavina, 2012). Weight-related teasing occurs in a variety of forms. Sometimes, overweight or obese students are called names like earthquake, fat ape girl, shamu, chubby, bubblebutt, and so forth. For example, when an overweight or obese student was jumping rope in the gymnasium, one of his peers said, "It is an earthquake." Sometimes, overweight or obese students are laughed at when they accidentally fall onto the ground during sports and physical activities. Sometimes, overweight or obese students are verbally teased for wearing certain types of clothing; awkward movements as a result of moving body parts such as breasts bouncing, belly fat shaking, and thighs rubbing; missing a hit during a baseball game; or showing poor skill performance and movements during fitness, sports, and games. Sometimes, overweight or obese students are "playfully" checked" (meaning insulted or made fun of) or joked about, where peers compare their body weight to that of a bulldozer. For example, one overweight or obese student reported a comment made by their peers about his moving body part: "You don't need to run because you are too big, your chest is too big. It will be hitting you in your face" (Li & Rukavina, 2012, p. 311). At other times, overweight or obese students physically confront their peers as a result of being teased. For example, one overweight or obese male student reported that he got into a fight with another boy because that boy called him "tubbo." In another situation, an overweight or obese student became too tired while playing sports and wanted to take a break. His peers got mad at him and made negative comments. They even physically pushed and flipped him (Li & Rukavina, 2012). Among these various forms of teasing, the most frequently occurring types among those interviewed in particular were playful checking and negative comments with regards to overweight or obese students' skills and movements during fitness activities, sports, and games. For example, one overweight or obese student reported, "When I cannot do the push-ups, pull-ups, and running, they would comment '(I am) too fat to do it'" (Li & Rukavina, 2012, p. 311).

Overweight or obese students experience obesity bias not only from their peers but also from their teachers in physical education (PE) classes (Bauer et al., 2004; Greenleaf & Weiller, 2005; Li & Rukavina, 2012; Peterson, Puhl, & Luedicke, 2012). In-service PE teachers express negative attitudes toward overweight students, set low learning expectations for overweight students, laugh at negative comments by other students, and make disparaging comments and jokes about overweight students in class (Bauer et al., 2004; Greenleaf & Weiller, 2005; Peterson et al., 2012). For example, when an overweight or obese student was teased in the gym, a teacher made negative comments to other students, "Yeah, look at her. She looks nasty, trifling little girl, just trifling. She probably doesn't have any manners." Another overweight or obese student reported,

> We had a game one day. There was a whole bunch of people there and you have to run to the next base. They were like "look at her fat ass. That is why you guys are losing the game." I looked over at my coach and he like don't say nothing . . . don't say nothing. My coach was laughing at it.

Where Does Obesity Bias Occur in Physical Education?

In physical education classes, obesity bias occurs in different contexts at every corner of the gym (Li & Rukavina, 2012). Overweight or obese students are teased in the locker room while changing clothes. Sometimes, they are teased while sitting on bleachers or sitting out due to physical injury. During warm-up activities and fitness exercises, overweight or obese students are teased for running slow and not being able to do push-ups and sit-ups. During sports/games, overweight or obese students are teased because they missed a ball or hit a ball in the wrong direction. Consequently, overweight or obese students are often excluded from participating in these sports/games. The dynamics and nature of obesity bias can vary in these different locations. In some situations, the teasing may only involve one or two negative comments by a few peers and then desist. In other situations, one student may start the teasing and then followers will be all up in the face of overweight or obese students.

What Are the Consequences of Obesity Bias?

Obesity bias has negative implications for emotional well-being and health behaviors in children and adolescents (Bauer et al., 2004; Fox & Edmunds, 2000; Li & Rukavina, 2012; Pierce &

Wardle, 1997; Trout & Graber, 2009). These negative effects that overweight or obese students suffer from can be seen across all races and ethnic groups, are severe, and persevere in multiple facets (Eisenberg, Neumark-Sztainer, & Perry, 2003). Research shows that overweight or obese children who experience obesity bias and stigma internalize negative attitudes, and in turn they express bias and stigma against their in-group (Schwartz, Varaanian, Nosek, & Brownell, 2006). The negative effects of obesity bias are more detrimental when overweight students internalize bias and stigma (Hilbert, Braehler, Haeuser, & Zenger, 2014). Overweight or obese individuals who internalize bias and stigma often exhibit more frequent binge-eating behaviors, refuse to diet or exercise, and show lower core self-evaluation (Hilbert et al., 2014; Puhl & Latner, 2007).

Obesity bias has negative impacts on emotional well-being in children and adolescents (Brownell et al., 2005; Eisenberg et al., 2006; Haines et al., 2006; Puhl, 2011; Puhl & Brownell, 2001). Overweight or obese children and adolescents who are targets of obesity bias and stigma are more likely to show low levels of self-esteem, have high levels of depression, be socially isolated, have suicidal attempts, and engage in self-blame for their negative social experiences (Brownell et al., 2005; Eisenberg et al., 2006; Haines et al., 2006; Puhl, 2011; Puhl & Brownell, 2001). Obesity bias also has negative implications for health behaviors in children and adolescents. Research has shown that overweight or obese students who suffer obesity bias during physical activities enjoy sports less; prefer isolated, sedentary activities (Hayden-Wade et al., 2005); have higher levels of unhealthy behaviors such as prolonged television watching, playing video games, and eating junk food (Gortmaker et al., 1996); and display lower physical activity levels than their non-overweight or obese peers (Faith et al., 2002; Storch et al., 2007). Obesity bias can serve as a barrier that prevents overweight or obese children and adolescents from developing and maintaining a healthy, physically active lifestyle (Bauer, Yang, & Austin, 2004; Faith et al., 2002). As a result of the sufferings of obesity bias, overweight or obese children and adolescents might resist any lifestyle interventions that focus on the promotion of a healthy, physically active lifestyle (Bosch, Stradmeijer, & Seidell, 2004).

In school physical education, overweight or obese students also experience serious psychological, behavioral, and emotional consequences as a result of obesity bias. The severity of the psychological, behavioral, and emotional damage ranges from feeling uncomfortable to attempting suicide. The negative impacts not only affect their learning and engagement in physical education, but go beyond to affect their daily lives. Overweight or obese students who are teased are more likely than other children to:

- Feel bad about themselves
- Feel unappreciated, like nobody wants them around
- Feel uncomfortable in physical education class
- Be excluded from activities/sports
- Exhibit learned helplessness
- Express a preference for isolated, sedentary activities
- Enjoy sports less
- Be less engaged in physical activity or even avoid participation in activities in physical education
- Feel sad and left out
- Feel hurt
- Cry
- Try to do everything to fit in with their peers
- Feel the pressure to lose weight to look good
- Feel depressed and annoyed at the same time
- Think about suicide
- Intentionally hurt themselves

- Be absent from school and dislike school
- Have lower academic achievement

For example, one overweight or obese student reported how obesity biases affect her. She said,

> I felt bad . . . really bad, like sometimes when they check me now. When I was younger, I used to get real mad, and go home upset. I used to not go to sleep. I used to not want to go to school. I didn't want to go anywhere because I always thought that I am fat and ugly, nobody wants to talk to me, and I will never have a boyfriend. Those people made my self-esteem low . . . real low. I also used to do some crazy stuff because I used to think I was no good. I was never going to be nothing. I will have no friends.

When this overweight or obese student was asked to elaborate on the crazy things that she has done, she said,

> I remember one time that I was real mad. Somebody had checked me real bad. I would go home and start choking myself. I was trying to kill myself because I just didn't want to be here. I thought I wasn't going to be nothing in life. I didn't want to be here because I didn't think anybody would ever like me, so that's why I tried to kill myself. I would stab, cut myself, and stick myself or whatever, to take the pain away. However, that didn't do nothing but cause more pain. So I see that didn't work and I would try another method.

The voices of these overweight or obese students shall be heard by their peers and physical education teachers. Students and physical education teachers shall be aware of their bias and stigma toward overweight or obese students, and realize the negative implications of their attitudes, comments, and behaviors regarding overweight or obese students. Why do non-overweight or obese students and physical education teachers need to know overweight or obese students' negative psychosocial and emotional experiences in physical education? Knowing about the suffering of overweight or obese students can help physical eduation teachers and non-overweight or obese students develop empathy toward overweight or obese students. The invoking of empathy can be an effective way to reduce obesity bias and stigmatizing beliefs among physical education teachers and peers. It can also help physical education teachers develop teaching strategies to create positive experiences and eliminate negative experiences among overweight or obese students. Positive experiences can increase overweight or obese students' motivation, engagement, and learning in physical education. Policies and program interventions can also be developed and implemented to address obesity bias and its negative consequences in physical education and for the entire school. A whole-school approach with policies and program interventions involving all students, faculty, and staff member can effectively reduce or eliminate the bias and stigmatizing beliefs about overweight or obese students.

Conceptual Frameworks for Obesity Bias Reduction

Researchers have proposed several conceptual frameworks to guide program interventions on obesity bias reduction in physical education settings (Rukavina & Li, 2008; Rukavina, Li, Bo, & Sun, 2010). These conceptual frameworks are attribution theory, consciousness raising, perspective taking/evoking empathy, receptivity/size acceptance, perceived social consensus, and experiential learning. In this section, we will briefly describe each of these conceptual frameworks so that PE teachers and PE teacher educators at higher education institutions can have a theoretical foundation. This can help them gain a better understanding of the strategies that are presented in the next section.

According to attribution theory (Weiner, 1986), students can attribute the causes of success and failure to either personally uncontrollable factors such as ability or controllable factors such as effort in achievement contexts. Ascribing failures to relatively uncontrollable variables is associated with maladaptive motivational and behavioral responses such as lower performances, showing less effort, or easily giving up. On the other hand, attributing failures to more controllable variables is associated with adaptive motivational and behavioral responses such as more persistence and effort, and performance improvement following failure (Weiner, 1986).

Attribution theory has been applied to the study of obesity and obesity bias issues. According to attribution theory, individuals can attribute the causes of obesity to either personally controllable factors such as diet and exercise or uncontrollable factors such as genetics and environment. Obesity bias occurs when individuals attribute others' being overweight or obese to personally controllable factors. They view overweight or obese individuals as being responsible for their body weight and blame them for being overweight or obese. The assignment of blame affects the degree to which a person is willing to endorse positive or negative attitudes toward overweight or obese individuals. Consequently, these attitudes will influence his or her willingness to socially interact with overweight or obese individuals. As argued by Crandall (1994), obesity bias is rooted in an ideology of blaming. People perceive that overweight or obese individuals are responsible for their body weight. The general public acknowledges that the etiology of obesity is complex and numerous factors can cause obesity, including genetics, personal lifestyle factors, physical and social environments, and so forth; however, people still view a person's weight as being largely determined by diet and exercises. Most people believe that if someone is overweight or obese, it is her or his fault because she or he is not being responsible, lacks willpower and motivation, or is simply lazy. As a result, people develop bias and stigmatizing beliefs about overweight or obese individuals without knowing the nature of the problem.

To avoid the development of obesity bias, it is best to educate the public to understand the complex etiology of obesity and direct the public to attribute obesity to personally uncontrollable factors such as genetics and physical and social environments. Providing information about the nature of controllability of body weight can have an impact on a person's attitude toward overweight or obese individuals. Research in this area has shown a mixed pattern of results. Some studies successfully reduced explicit obesity bias among adults (Crandall, 1994; Puhl, Schwartz, & Brownell 2005) by convincing participants that obesity is not caused by lack of self-control and willpower but is attributed to uncontrollable factors such as genetics and metabolism. Other studies were able to change students' beliefs about the controllability of obesity; however, they failed to reduce obesity bias toward overweight or obese peers (Anesbury & Tiggerman, 2000; Bell & Morgan, 2000). It appears that providing information about the uncontrollability of obesity can reduce obesity bias; however, the effect is minimal.

Consciousness raising is another conceptual framework that has been proposed for bias reduction (Chambliss, Finley, & Blair, 2004; Greenwald & Banaji, 1995; Neumark-Sztainer, Story, & Harris, 1999). Students are often unaware that they possess bias toward overweight or obese individuals. When environmental cues present themselves, students can unconsciously express obesity bias. For example, when a person tells a fat joke, students will naturally laugh at it. Consciousness raising makes students aware that cultural implicit biases exist, and they occur on the unconscious level. This allows students to become aware of their predispositions toward overweight or obese students and the environmental cues that could elicit their discriminatory behaviors.

Under the conceptual framework of consciousness raising, individuals are provided with information about the nature and different types of obesity, its pervasiveness, and environmental cues where obesity bias can be activated. When people are cognizant of their obesity bias and recognize the environmental cues, they potentially can catch themselves before displaying any biased behavior toward overweight or obese individuals. Rukavina, Li, and Rowell (2008) conducted a study to elicit kinesiology preprofessionals' consciousness about obesity bias through a classroom lecture and discussions, a group activity on the barriers to healthy lifestyles following the lecture/discussion, and a service-learning project, with the goal of reducing their explicit anti-fat attitudes. The findings showed that participants' anti-fat attitudes concerning whether overweight or obese people are responsible for their body weight (blame/control subscale) was significantly reduced through consciousness-raising and service-learning interventions. The partial success in bias reduction in their study suggests that future endeavors may need to first make participants aware of their bias toward overweight or obese people, and then combine other strategies to have a better chance of reducing obesity bias.

Perspective taking/evoking empathy toward a member of a stigmatized group has also been suggested as one mechanism to reduce obesity bias (Gapinski, Schwartz, & Brownell, 2006; Teachman et al., 2003). Under this conceptual framework, students will hear or read a story about an overweight or obese individual talking about his or her stigmatized experiences as well as the associated psychosocial and emotional sufferings that he or she experiences. Students can also perform a role-playing activity by assuming that they are overweight or obese, and trying to imagine the feelings that they would suffer as a result of being teased. Through these perspective-taking activities, students can feel empathy toward overweight or obese individuals by putting themselves into a similar situation as these individuals. Subsequently, students can change their feelings and develop positive attitudes toward overweight or obese individuals.

Several researchers have employed perspective-taking/evoking-empathy strategies in order to reduce obesity bias; however, the findings were mixed (Gapinski et al., 2006; Teachman et al., 2003; Wiese, Wilson, Jones, & Neises, 1992). In a study by Teachman and colleagues (2003), 90 adult women were asked to read a first-person account of the stigmatized experiences of an obese individual, think about the feelings of that individual, and then write an essay to elaborate on their feelings. Those components were likely to induce empathy toward the obese young woman. However, the results showed that evoking empathy failed to produce lower implicit or explicit bias in women with lower BMI. In another study by Gapinski and colleagues (2006), participants watched a video of the victim, and they did not report any significant change in their obesity bias. On the other hand, Wiese and colleagues (1992) designed an intervention to reduce negative stereotypes of obese people based on the elaboration likelihood model (Petty & Cacioppo, 1986). Empathy was evoked by having medical students watch a video of an obese nurse talking about the stigmatized experience that she encountered, participating in two role-playing exercises where they took the perspectives of an obese person, and reading materials discussing the causes of obesity. The results showed that evoking empathy reduced negative attitudes in medical students.

La Greca and Bearman (2000) have argued that instead of providing information that makes obese people appear non-normal, interventions need to be designed to influence deep-seated stereotypes or implicit obesity bias by providing positive information about obese students to enhance receptivity/size acceptance. Individuals' receptivity may have increased if they had been provided with positive information about the overweight or obese individuals, such as a sport or academic subject that they are good at. Little research has been conducted to examine the efficacy of counterproductive conditions to effectively reduce obesity bias against overweight or obese people. Recently, Gapinski et al. (2006) attempted to reduce implicit and explicit bias against overweight or obese people by using media-based empathy and counterconditioning (counterproductive conditions). The interventions, however, failed to reduce both implicit and explicit bias. As suggested by the authors, the failure might be due to the ordering between priming and conditioning videos or that the participants viewed both videos. Other research focusing on the promotion of size acceptance has shown a successful bias reduction (Hague & White, 2005; Irving, 2000). For example, in Hague and White's (2005) study, a web-based educational module focusing on size acceptance was developed and implemented to change student teachers' and school teachers' obesity bias. Even though there were a couple of methodological limitations (i.e., failure to establish intervention fidelity and short intervention duration), the findings showed that participants' negative attitudes toward overweight or obese individuals in the intervention group decreased significantly.

Perceived social consensus model assumes that a person's attitude is influenced by his or her perceptions of other people's stereotypical and stigmatizing beliefs (Stangor, Sechrist, & Jost, 2001a, 2001b). Individuals can affiliate and obtain membership, social support, acceptance, and security in social groups as a result of sharing similar attitudes and beliefs (Baumeister & Leary, 1995; Levine, Resnick, & Higgins, 1993; Stangor & Crandall, 2000; Stangor & Schaller, 2000). Attitude change is more likely to occur when information comes from a social group that they identify with and value (Haslam et al., 1996; Haslam et al., 1999; Stangor et al., 2001a, 2001b). Social consensus information can affect the development of obesity bias, especially if a person values an in-group membership and feels a strong need for group acceptance. Researchers have examined the effectiveness of bias reduction by employing the perceived social consensus model to emphasize favorable attitudes and beliefs about overweight or obese individuals among members of valued social groups. The findings from this line of research showed an improvement of attitudes and a bias reduction (Puhl, Schwartz, & Brownell, 2005).

What Should Physical Education Teachers Do When Obesity Bias Occurs in Their Classes?

Obesity bias is prevalent and perseveres in physical education, which presents an unprecedented challenge for physical education teachers to address this issue in their classes. Physical education teachers lack not only awareness of obesity bias, but also knowledge and skills to address this serious issue in their classes. So, what should physical education teachers do when obesity bias occurs in their classes? They should not use exercises as a punishment for the teaser by making him or her do push-ups on the bleachers or run on the track. Using exercises as a punishment will not solve the issue and oftentimes leads to an increase in teasing toward overweight or obese students. Physical education teachers should not ignore the teasing incidents, laugh at them, or even make disparaging comments or jokes about the students. The following strategies are recommended for physical education teachers to handle obesity bias:

- Step in to stop the teasing or checking right away. Have a conversation with the teasers about negative implications of their behaviors toward their peers.
- Communicate the incidents to a school counselor who can take further actions. A school counselor can hold a follow-up meeting with students and parents if needed.

- Write students up or send them to the principal's office.
- Respond consistently and appropriately to any incident of obesity bias without showing favoritism.
- Work with the school counselor to provide referrals to mental health professionals.

What Preventive Strategies Can Physical Education Teachers Use to Reduce or Eliminate Obesity Bias?

Besides the aforementioned reactive strategies that physical education teachers can employ to handle obesity bias as it occurs, a variety of preventive strategies are available. A teacher can make a difference by becoming aware of his or her own obesity bias, developing empathy, and working to address the needs and concerns of overweight or obese students in physical education. The mastery and successful implementation of these preventive strategies can help physical education teachers create a positive, inclusive learning environment, where obesity bias and stigma can be reduced or eliminated.

Preventive Strategies for Physical Education Teachers to Reduce or Eliminate Their Own Bias

Teachers' attitudes are an important determinant of their behaviors, and teachers' attitudes and behaviors can shape students' attitudes and behaviors (Stelzer, 2005). Research shows that many physical education teachers possess obesity bias toward overweight or obese students (Bauer et al., 2004; Greenleaf & Weiller, 2005; Li & Rukavina, 2012; Peterson et al., 2012). This bias can negatively impact how physical education teachers treat overweight or obese students in their classes. To create a bias-free learning environment, physical education teachers must not possess any bias or stigmatizing beliefs themselves. To address obesity bias, it is important for physical education teachers to demonstrate appropriate attitudes and teaching behaviors toward overweight or obese students. Therefore, it is critical for physical education teachers to identify their own personal biases and stigmatizing behaviors, and then challenge them through attitude and behavioral interventions. Physical education teachers can ask themselves the following questions to evaluate whether they have and/or display obesity bias and stigmatizing behaviors toward overweight or obese students.

- In my teaching, do I make negative assumptions regarding students' characteristics, personality, physical ability, and skills on the basis of their body weight?
- Do I feel comfortable teaching students of all shapes and sizes?
- Am I sensitive to the needs and concerns of overweight or obese students in my teaching?
- Do I allocate equal time and attention to overweight or obese students in my teaching?
- Am I willing to make adaptations to learning tasks to accommodate the needs of overweight or obese students in my teaching?

After coming to the realization that they are biased toward overweight or obese students, physical education teachers must educate themselves more about obesity bias and its negative impact on these students' psychosocial and emotional well-being. Physical education teachers must recognize that the etiology of obesity is complex and factors such as physical environments, parent–child relationship, genetics, social economic status, and prescription drug side effects all can cause obesity, thus avoiding any stereotypical beliefs that obesity is personally controllable. I is important to approach overweight or obese students with sensitivity as they may suffer from many psychological, emotional, and behavioral damages from perceived obesity bias. During physical education classes, teachers must consciously be aware of their language, and make plans to address the concerns and needs of overweight or obese students without bringing undue attention. Upon the completion of each physical education lesson, instructors must conduct critical reflections on their teaching to identify any possible incident where they could display bias toward overweight or obese students.

Preventive Strategies to Reduce or Eliminate Obesity Bias and Stigma among Students

To reduce or eliminate obesity bias and stigma among students, physical education teachers can incorporate a variety of preventive strategies in their classes.

- For the majority of teasing incidents, physical education teachers are either not present or do not notice the teasing. Physical education teachers must actively supervise students so that they are present at the time of teasing.
- Many physical education teachers are not aware of obesity bias occurring in their classes. They must raise their awareness level, pay attention to the dynamics of students' interactions in their classes, and allocate more quality time and attention to overweight or obese students.
- Teasing very often occurs on the bleachers and in the locker rooms. Physical education teachers must be mindful of these hidden locations and increase their supervision in these locations. Knowing where and when overweight students are teased helps teachers to stategically allocate their attention to these areas and stop teasing at the moment when it occurs.

- Educate students that the etiology of obesity is complex, and obesity is often not under a person's control. Overweight or obese students are often blamed for their weight conditions because the general public holds a strong belief that obesity is caused by personally controllable factors. Physical education teachers can educate students to recognize the complexity of obesity and that there are multiple reasons for obesity other than dieting and physical activity. Factors such as physical environments, parent–child relationship, genetics, social economic status, and medication side effects all can cause obesity. Students should be taught to avoid stereotypical beliefs that obesity is personally controllable. Our society should also be responsible for the epidemic of obesity rather than overweight or obese individuals since it has created a toxic environment for people to live in by making junk food so readily available and mass producing and marketing it to children.

- Evoke empathy in students. First, physical education teachers can have students listen to overweight or obese students talk about their negative experience. Then physical education teachers can have students discuss their feelings and thoughts. At the end of discussions, physical education teachers can conclude that students shall treat all people the same and with respect and that teasing is something students should not do since it causes damage to overweight or obese students' emotional well-being (e.g., feeling sad, invisible, hurt, depressed, lower self-worth, lower self-esteem).

- Have students participate in role-playing activities. Students will first make a list of obesity bias examples they have witnessed, put themselves in overweight or obese students' situation, and then speculate how they would feel and why the bias made them feel that way.

- Have students perform role-play activities to enhance receptivity (La Greca & Bearman, 2000). For example, ask students to think of a close friend or a family member who is overweight or obese and then ask, What sport skills and academic subjects is this person good at? What special talents does he or she have? What tasks does he or she value? Do you value these tasks too?

- Educate students that overweight or obese students have their own special gifts. Every student has his or her own gifted areas. Overweight or obese students may not be good at physical or fitness activities, but they may possess other talents that non-overweight or non-obese students do not have. Overweight or obese students might be good at playing sports such as basketball or football, singing, dancing, acting, cooking, drawing, or science and math, or they may possess tech-savvy skills. They are also smart and diligent. Some overweight or obese students place a high value on respecting other people, being nice to others and making good grades. They might value going to church, hanging out with friends, and doing one's best. These tasks that overweight or obese students value are very important values for all of us to live in today's society.

- Educate students that overweight or obese students have strong wills. Even though it is very hard for overweight or obese students to lose weight and they struggle to achieve their goals, they do have strong wills because they don't give up and try hard to do whatever they need to do.

- Work with school counselors and administrators to develop a school-wide no-bias/teasing/bullying policy. This policy prohibits any bias, teasing, and bullying of any student in school or cyberbullying outside of the school. The policy should provide a clear definition of bias, teasing, and bullying; consequences of violations; and a procedure for reporting, documenting, and investigating any bias, teasing, and bullying incidents. Physical education teachers can post this policy in the locker room, inside their office, and inside gym. Students and parents should be made aware of this policy, its associated consequences, and the procedure for reporting a violation. Physical education teachers can make clear the view that obesity bias is not acceptable.

- Physical education teachers can allocate class time for students to share feelings and different viewpoints about body size and shape, thus promoting receptivity/size acceptance.
- Students are often unaware of their own bias and stigmatizing beliefs about overweight or obese peers. With support from school administrators, physical education teachers can collect data on obesity bias and discuss them with students in combination with lectures on obesity bias for consciousness raising. Physical education teachers can also integrate lessons on peer relationships and positive social behaviors into their instruction curriculum.
- Build a positive, caring learning community where students can develop positive attitudes, master effective social and problem-solving skills for interpersonal success, learn to respect each other, develop personal and social responsibility, build supportive relationships with each other, and care for each other. This positive, caring learning community can be an effective prevention program to reduce obesity bias among students. PE teachers can build a positive, caring learning community through innovative instructional/curricular models (i.e., adventure education, cooperative learning, and personal and social responsivity), providing

differentiated instructions, and building interpersonal rapport (Li, Rukavina, & Foster, 2013).

• Work with parent–teacher associations, school administrators and teachers, and community organizations to form a safety committee to coordinate and integrate obesity bias prevention efforts (Tingstrom, 2015).

Summary

Obesity bias in physical education classes occurs frequently at every corner and has serious consequences on overweight or obese students' psychosocial, emotional, and behavioral well-being. Physical education teachers, as agents of change, must first be aware of the existence of obesity bias in physical education and its serious consequences. The knowledge of obesity bias and psychosocial and emotional suffering of overweight or obese students in physical education can evoke empathy among teachers and help them to strategically design policies, programs, and teaching pedagogies to reduce obesity bias and its negative impact on overweight or obese students. Through creating a positive, caring learning community, physical education teachers can maximize overweight or obese students' motivation, engagement, and learning in physical education.

This chapter provided numerous preventive and reactive strategies that physical education teachers can use to handle obesity bias. Given the resilience of implicit bias and the complexity and difficulty of changing stigmatizing beliefs or bias, it seems unlikely that a single strategy can successfully reduce bias against overweight or obese people. A comprehensive school-wide and long-term approach targeting multiple sources at multiple levels should be employed to reduce or even eliminate obesity bias in schools in the future (Gapinski et al., 2006; Haines et al., 2006; Puhl, Schwartz, & Brownell, 2005). It is recommended that physicial education teachers make students aware of their obesity bias (consciousness raising) before implementing any other bias reduction strategies.

References

Anesbury, T., & Tiggerman, M. (2000). An attempt to reduce negative stereotyping of obesity in children by changing controllability beliefs. *Health Education Research, 15*, 145–152.

Bauer, K. W., Yang, Y. W., & Austin, S. B. (2004). "How can we stay healthy when you're throwing all of this in front of us?" Findings from focus groups and interviews in middle schools on environment influences on nutrition and physical activity. *Health Education and Behavior, 31*, 34–46.

Baumeister, R. F., & Leary, M. R. (1995). The need to belong: Desire for interpersonal attachments as a fundamental human motivation. *Psychological Bulletin, 117*, 497–529.

Bell, S. K., & Morgan, S. B. (2000). Children's attitudes and behavioral intentions toward a peer presented as obese: Does a medical explanation for the obesity make a difference? *Journal of Pediatric Psychology, 25*, 137–145.

Bosch, J., Stradmeijer, M., & Seidell, J. (2004). Psychosocial characteristics of obese children/youngsters and their families: Implications for preventive and curative interventions. *Patient Education and Counseling, 55*(3), 353–362.

Brownell, K. D., Puhl, R., Schwartz, M. B., & Rudd, L. (Eds.). (2005). *Weight bias: Nature, consequences, and remedies.* New York: Guilford Publications.

Chambliss, H. O., Finley, C. E., & Blair, S. N. (2004). Attitudes toward obese individuals among exercise science students. *Medicine & Science in Sports & Exercise, 36*(3), 468–474.

Cothran, D. J., & Ennis, C. D. (1999). Alone in a crowd: Meeting students' needs for relevance and connection in urban high school physical education. *Journal of Teaching in Physical Education, 18*, 234–247.

Cramer, P., & Steinwert, T. (1998). Thin is good, fat is bad: How early does it begin? *Journal of Applied Developmental Psychology, 19*, 429–451.

Crandall, C. S. (1994). Prejudice against fat people: Ideology and self-interest. *Journal of Personality and Social Psychology, 66*, 882–894.

Eisenberg, M. E., Neumark-Sztainer, D., Haines, J., & Wall, M. (2006). Weight-teasing and emotional well-being in adolescents: Longitudinal findings from project EAT. *Journal of Adolescent Health, 28*, 675–683.

Eisenberg, M. E., Neumark-Sztainer, D., & Perry, C. L. (2003). Peer harassment, school connectedness, and academic achievement. *Journal of School Health, 73*, 311–316.

Ennis, C. D., Cothran, D. J., Stockin, K. D., Owens, L. M., Loftus, S. J., Swanson, L., & Hopsicker, P. (1997). Implementing a curriculum in a context of fear and disengagement. *Journal of Teaching in Physical Education, 17*, 58–72.

Ennis, C. D., Solmon, M. A., Satina, B., Loftus, S. J., Mensch, J., & McCauley, M. T. (1999). Creating a sense of family in urban schools using the "sport for peace" curriculum. *Research Quarterly for Exercise and Sport, 70*, 273–285.

Faith, M. S., Leone, M. A., Ayers, T. S., Heo, M., & Pietrobelli, A. (2002). Weight criticism during physical activity, coping skills, and reported physical activity in children. *Pediatrics, 110*, e23.

Fox, K. R., & Edmunds, L. D. (2000). Understanding the world of the "fat kid": Schools help provide a better experience? *Reclaiming Child Youth, 9*, 177–181.

Gapinski, K. D., Schwartz, M. B., & Brownell, K. D. (2006). Can television change anti-fat attitudes and behavior? *Journal of Applied Biobehavioral Research, 11*, 1–28.

Gortmaker, S. H., Must, A., Sobol, A. M., Peterson, K., Coldite, G. A., & Dietz, W. H. (1996). Television viewing as a cause of increasing obesity among children in the United States, 1986–1990. *Archives of Pediatrics and Adolescent Medicine, 150*, 356–362.

Greenleaf, C., & Weiller, K. (2005). Perceptions of youth obesity among physical educators. *Social Psychology of Education, 8*, 407–423.

Greenwald, A. G., & Banaji, M. R. (1995). Implicit social cognition: Attitudes, self-esteem, and stereotypes. *Psychology Review, 102*(1), 4–27.

Hague, A. L., & White, A. A. (2005). Web-based intervention for changing attitudes of obesity among current and future teachers. *Journal of Nutrition Education and Behavior, 37*(2), 58–66.

Haines, J., Neumark-Sztainer, D., Eisenberg, M. E., & Hannan, P. J. (2006). Weight teasing and disordered eating behaviors in adolescents: Longitudinal findings from project EAT (eating among teens). *Pediatrics, 117*(2), 209–215.

Haslam, S. A., Oakes, P. J., McGarty, C., Turner, J. C., Reynolds, K. J., & Eggins, R. A. (1996). Stereotyping and social influence: The mediation of stereotype applicability and sharedness by the views of in-group and out-group members. *British Journal of Social Psychology, 35*, 369–397.

Haslam, S. A., Oakes, P. J., Reynolds, K. J., & Turner, J. C. (1999). Social identity salience and the emergence of stereotype consensus. *Personality and Social Psychology Bulletin, 25*, 809–818.

Hayden-Wade, H. A., Stein, R. I., Ghaderi, A., Saelens, B. E., Zabinski, M. F., & Wilfley, D. E. (2005). Prevalence, characteristics, and correlates of teasing experiences among overweight children vs. non-overweight peers. *Obesity Research, 13*(8), 1381–1392.

Hilbert, A., Braehler, E., Haeuser, W., & Zenger, M. (2014). Weight bias internalization, core self-evaluation, and health in overweight and obese persons. *Obesity, 22*, 79–85.

Irving, L. (2000). Promoting size acceptance in elementary school children: The EDAP puppet program. *International Journal of Eating Disorder, 8*, 221–232.

Janssen, I., Craig, W. M., Boyce, W. F., & Pickett, W. (2004). Association between overweight and obesity within bullying behaviors in school-aged children. *Pediatrics, 113*, 1187–1194.

Klaczynski, P. A., Daniel, D. B., & Keller, P. S. (2009). Appearance idealization, body esteem, causal attributions, and ethnic variations in the development of obesity stereotypes. *Journal of Applied Developmental Psychology, 30*, 537–551. doi: 10.1016/j.appdev.2008.12.031

La Greca, A. M., & Bearman, K. J. (2000). Commentary: Children with pediatric conditions: Can peers' impressions be managed? And what about their friends? *Journal of Pediatric Psychology, 25*(3), 147–149.

Levine, J. M., Resnick, L. B., & Higgins, E. T. (1993). Social foundations of cognition. *Annual Review of Psychology, 44*, 585–612.

Li, W., & Rukavina, P. (2012). The nature, occurring contexts, and psychological implications of weight-related teasing in urban physical education programs. *Research Quarterly for Exercise and Sport, 83*(2), 308–317.

Li, W., Rukavina, P., & Foster, C. (2013). Overweight or obese students' perceptions of caring in urban physical education programs. *Journal of Sport Behavior, 36*, 189–203.

Margulies, A. S., Floyd, R. G., & Hojnoski, R. L. (2008). Body size stigmatization: An examination of attitudes of African-American preschool-age children attending Head Start. *Journal of Pediatric Psychology, 33*, 487–496.

Neumark-Sztainer, D., Story, M., & Faibisch, L. (1998). Perceived stigmatization among overweight African-American and Caucasian adolescent girls. *Journal of Adolescent Health, 23*, 264–270.

Neumark-Sztainer, D., Story, M., & Harris, T. (1999). Beliefs and attitudes about obesity among teachers and school health care providers working with adolescents. *Journal of Nutrition and Education, 31*, 3–9.

Peterson, J. L., Puhl, R. M., & Luedicke, J. (2012). An experimental assessment of physical educators' expectations and attitudes: The importance of student weight and gender. *Journal of School Health, 82,* 432–440.

Petty, R. E., & Cacioppo, J. T. (1986). The elaboration likelihood model of persuasion. In L. Berkowitz (Ed.), *Advances in experimental social psychology* (Vol. 19, pp. 123–205). New York: Academic Press.

Pierce, J. W., & Wardle, J. (1997). Cause and effect beliefs and self-esteem of overweight children. *Journal of Child Psychology and Psychiatry and Allied Disciplines, 38,* 645–650.

Puhl, R. M. (2011). Weight stigmatization toward youth: A significant problem in need of societal solutions. *Childhood Obesity, 7,* 359–363.

Puhl, R. M., & Brownell, K. D. (2001). Bias, discrimination, and obesity. *Obesity Research, 9,* 788–805.

Puhl, R. M., & Latner, J. D. (2007). Stigma, obesity, and the health of the nation's children. *Psychological Bulletin, 133,* 557–580.

Puhl, R. M., Schwartz, M. B., & Brownell, K. D. (2005). Impact of perceived consensus on stereotypes about obese people: A new approach for reducing bias. *Health Psychology, 24*(5), 517–525.

Rukavina, P., & Li, W. (2008). School physical activity interventions: Do not forget about obesity bias. *Obesity Reviews, 9,* 67–75.

Rukavina, P., Li, W., Bo, S., & Sun, H. (2010). A service learning based project to change implicit and explicit bias toward obese individuals in kinesiology pre-professionals. *Obesity Facts: The European Journal of Obesity, 3*(2), 117–152.

Rukavina, P., Li, W., & Rowell, M. (2008). A service learning based intervention to change attitudes toward obese individuals in kinesiology pre-professionals. *Social Psychology of Education: An International Journal, 11,* 95–112.

Schwartz, M. B., Varaanian, L. R., Nosek, B. A., & Brownell, K. D. (2006). The influence of one's own body weight on implicit and explicit anti-fat bias. *Obesity, 4,* 440–447.

Stangor, C., & Crandall, C. S. (2000). Threat and social construction of stigma. In T. F. Heatherton, R. E. Kleck, M. R. Hebl, & J. G. Hull (Eds.), *The social psychology of stigma* (pp. 62–87). New York: Guilford Press.

Stangor, C., & Schaller, M. (2000). Stereotypes as individual and collective representations. In C. Stangor (Ed.), *Stereotypes and prejudice: Essential readings* (pp. 64–82). Philadelphia, PA: Psychology Press, and Taylor & Francis.

Stangor, C., Sechrist, G. B., & Jost, J. T. (2001a). Changing beliefs by providing consensus information. *Personality and Social Psychology Bulletin, 27,* 486–496.

Stangor, C., Sechrist, G. B., & Jost, J. T. (2001b). Social influence and intergroup beliefs: The role of perceived social consensus. In J. P. Forgas & K. D. Williams (Eds.), *Social influence: Direct and indirect processes* (pp. 235–252). Philadelphia, PA: Psychology Press.

Stelzer, J. (2005). Promoting healthy lifestyles: Prescriptions for physical educators. *Journal of Physical Education, Recreation & Dance, 76*(4), 26–33.

Storch, E. A., Milsom, V. A., DeBraganza, N., Lewin, A. B., Geffken, G. R., & Silverstein, J. H. (2007). Peer victimization, psychosocial adjustment, and physical activity in overweight and at-risk-for-overweight youth. *Journal of Pediatric Psychology, 32*, 80–89.

Su, W., & Santo, A. D. (2011). Preschool children's perceptions of overweight peers. *Journal of Early Childhood Research, 10*, 19–31.

Tang-Peronard, J. L., & Heitmann, B. L. (2008). Stigmatization of obese children and adolescents: The importance of gender. *Obesity Reviews, 9*, 522–534.

Teachman, B. A., Gapinski, K. D., Brownell, K. D., & Rawlins, M. (2003). Demonstrations of implicit anti-fat bias: The impact of providing causal information and evoking empathy. *Health Psychology, 22*(1), 68–78.

Tingstrom, C. A. (2015). Addressing the needs of overweight students in elementary physical education: Creating an environment of care and success. *Strategies, 28*(1), 8–12.

Trout, J., & Graber, K. C. (2009). Perceptions of overweight students concerning their experience in physical education. *Journal of Teaching in Physical Education, 28*, 272–292.

U.S. Department of Health and Human Services. (1996). *Physical activity and health: A report of the surgeon general.* Atlanta, GA: Author.

Weiner, B. (1986). *An attributional theory of motivation and emotion.* New York: Springer-Verlag.

Wiese, H. J., Wilson, J. F., Jones, R. A., & Neises, M. (1992). Obesity stigma reduction in medical students. *International Journal of Obesity and Related Metabolic Disorders, 16*(11), 859–868.

3

TEACHING STUDENTS HOW TO COPE WITH OBESITY BIAS

Overweight or obese students who are teased in physical education classes can suffer serious psychosocial, emotional, and behavioral damage. However, not all students are affected by obesity bias (Eisenberg, Neumark-Sztainer, Haines, & Wall, 2006; Li & Rukavina, 2012). Many factors—such as family ties, personality/traits, body image/body satisfaction levels, and coping mechanisms—can mediate the negative effects of obesity bias on overweight or obese students' psychosocial, emotional, and behavioral well-being (Faith et al., 2002; Mellin et al., 2002; Parker & Endler, 1992). Some overweight or obese students can use adaptive strategies to successfully cope with the stress produced by obesity bias and stigmatizing behaviors (Neumark-Sztainer, et al., 1998).

In this chapter, I will first define the term *coping* and describe the features of coping. Next, I will present strategies that overweight or obese students have used successfully to cope with obesity bias. This is followed by offering an instructional module for instructors to teach overweight or obese students how to cope against obesity bias. In the final section, I will provide advice to parents of overweight or obese students on how to handle sensitive issues when their children experience obesity bias at school. The main goal of this chapter is to equip physical education teachers, overweight or obese students, and students' parents and families with strategies to deal with obesity bias situations, thus reducing the degree of negative effects of stigma and obesity bias on overweight or obese students' overall health and well-being.

What Is Coping?

According to the theory of stress and coping, cognitive appraisal and coping mediate the effects of stressful events on immediate and long-term outcomes (Folkman, Lazarus, Dunkel-Schetter, DeLongis, & Gruen, 1986). Cognitive appraisal involves a process through which a person makes judgments about whether a particular life event can affect his or her well-being and if it does so, to what degree. Cognitive appraisal is composed of two main components—primary appraisal and secondary appraisal. Primary appraisal is a process in which one evaluates whether his or her well-being is at stake in a particular situation. In secondary appraisal, one makes judgments about what actions he or she can take to prevent or overcome the possibility of any harm or loss, or to improve the possibility of gaining any mastery or benefits (Folkman et al., 1986).

Coping is defined as a person's endeavor to deal with distress in the face of stressful life events (Lazarus & Folkman, 1984). Coping can regulate stressful emotions and modify the person–environment transaction process that produces the distress. Numerous factors, such as personal characteristics and social environments, determine how one confronts, responds to, and resolves stressful life events (Pierce, Sarason, & Sarason, 1996). Coping has three main features. First, coping is process oriented. It focuses on how a person thinks and what a person does in a particular stressful event, and how that can change as the stressful event unfolds itself. Second, coping is context specific in that it is shaped by particular individual and specific situations in which the stressful event occurs. Third, no assumption of what consists of good or bad coping is made prior to the stressful event. Coping simply refers to an individual's efforts to regulate emotional demands or alter the person–environment transaction in a stressful life event (Folkman et al., 1986; Lazarus & Folkman, 1984).

Coping mechanisms can potentially buffer overweight or obese students from the sufferings or reduce the negative effects of obesity bias on their psychosocial, emotional, and behavioral well-being. Numerous coping strategies are available for overweight or obese students to deal with weight-related bias and stigma in physical education classes. The effectiveness of coping is a function of complex interactions of situational and individual factors, such as group dynamics, specific occurring contexts, gender, race, personality, and previous coping experiences. Some coping strategies such as crying or listening to music can be beneficial for overweight or obese students to reduce their levels of distress. Other coping methods such as taking drugs or engaging in binge eating can only make their situation worse by further exacerbating obesity bias. In next section, I present a number of strategies that have been used by overweight or obese students to cope with obesity bias.

Mechanisms and Strategies for Coping with Obesity Bias

Overweight or obese students have made use of different mechanisms to cope with obesity bias when they experience teasing or bullying by teachers and peers in physical education.

Li, Rukavina, and Wright (2012) interviewed 47 overweight or obese students to investigate how they coped with obesity bias. The authors reported seven different coping mechanisms used by overweight or obese adolescents, including avoidance/psychological disengagement, social support, confrontation, stress reduction, self-protection, losing weight, and compensation. Under each of these coping mechanisms, a variety of strategies were used by overweight or obese adolescents to cope with obesity bias.

These coping strategies can be classified as reactive versus preventive. Reactive strategies are what overweight or obese students use to cope with obesity bias at the moment when it occurs. Preventive strategies are what overweight or obese students do to buffer themselves from being teased or bullied. These preventive strategies can be classified as adaptive versus maladaptive. Adaptive strategies are defined as coping responses that are beneficial to the well-being of overweight or obese students. On the other hand, maladaptive strategies consist of coping responses that can cause damage to the well-being of overweight or obese students. Having knowledge of these coping mechanisms and strategies can help physical education teachers select adaptive, reactive, and preventive ones to teach their overweight or obese students so that they can be better educated to successfully cope with obesity bias or weight-related teasing.

Avoidance and Psychological Disengagement

Avoidance and psychological disengagement is a mechanism that overweight or obese students can use to cope with obesity bias (for an in-depth review, see Li & Rukavina, 2009; Puhl & Brownell, 2003). When overweight or obese students are teased or bullied, they can ignore the teasing with silence or psychologically disengage themselves from the teasing event.

For example, one overweight or obese student reported, "I just ignored what they said. Just let them say what they wanted to say and don't worry about it." To prevent themselves from being teased or bullied, overweight or obese students can intentionally avoid the teaser or walk away from any situation where teasing can potentially occur. One overweight or obese student worried about being teased and tried to avoid the situation: "We had to jump rope and everything would just be bouncing. I would be too shy to do it in front of everybody. I would not do the jump rope. I would walk around or something because I was so shamed and knew that they would talk about me, saying like 'look at her stomach.'" Table 3.1 presents a number of avoidance and psychological disengagement coping strategies.

Seeking Social Support

Social support can act as a stress buffer (Barrera, 1986; Lakey & Cohen, 2000; Lakey & Drew, 1997). Seeking social support can

Table 3.1 Avoidance and Psychological Disengagement Coping Strategies Used by Overweight or Obese Students

1. Ignore what they say.
2. Do not think about what they are saying and try to forget what they say.
3. Walk away when they make the comments.
4. Change the subject by starting a new conversation with others.
5. Do not pay any attention and avoid showing any feelings.
6. Avoid teasers.
7. Do not look at the teasers and turn your head to look the other way.
8. Pretend that they did not say it.
9. Do not listen to them and brush it off your shoulder.
10. Self-talk to calm down.
11. Isolate yourself during negative interactions.

reduce the negative effects of obesity bias on overweight or obese students' well-being and help them develop better coping behaviors (Beehr & McGrath, 1992). Research shows that overweight or obese students often seek social support from their family members, teachers and school administrators, friends, or others to cope with weight-related teasing (Li et al., 2012). Overweight or obese students realize the importance of creating a network of friends who can be supportive and stand up for them in these stressful situations. The social support that overweight or obese students have received from their friends and/or peers has helped to stop teasing at the moment when it occurs. This support also helps them to get their emotions out, feel better, regain confidence, gain momentum, and buffer themselves from future teasing. One overweight or obese student commented that her friends were supportive and would say something to the teaser to stop teasing. Another overweight or obese student indicated that she felt much better after talking to her friend; she commented,

> I just gotta talk to my friends, you know, I would sit on the phone and talk to my girlfriend and something like that, you know, just kind of ease my mind of certain things that went on during the day, but I made it through. But other than that . . . I mean . . . that was the only person I really talk to about stuff like that . . . the only person I really felt comfortable talking to.

Another overweight or obese student said that making a lot of friends helped him out in situations, and these friends helped him to get better in sports and games, which stopped the teasing in the middle of the school year. He shared,

> Well, I'd made sure I got to know a lot of the kids, and I got them on my side . . . and they are my friends and stuff, and then they'd help me out sometimes when I wasn't doing very well. Also I'd make

sure I always tried my hardest and try to get stronger, faster, do something. And sometimes it would work. I would gradually get better at the games and things like that. . . . Well, like in the middle of the year, most of the bad teasing and stuff like that stopped.

The types of social support that overweight or obese students seek vary significantly in different ways. In some situations, overweight or obese students want to gain emotional support and confidence in themselves by talking about their negative experience and hurt feelings with family members and friends. In some situations, overweight or obese students seek not only emotional support to feel better, but also advice on how to deal with teasing. In other situations, overweight or obese students would like teachers/coaches and school administrators to step in and intervene with the teaser (Li et al., 2012).

Guided by social support as a coping mechanism, several coping strategies are presented in Table 3.2. Knowledge of these coping strategies can help physical education instructors select adaptive ones to teach to their students.

Confrontation

Overweight or obese students use confrontations as a mechanism to cope with obesity bias (Li et al., 2012). The types of confrontations used are dependent upon whether these students

Table 3.2 Coping Strategies with Social Support as a Mechanism

1. Create a network of friends who can be on your side and stand up for you when you are teased.
2. Talk to coaches/physical education teachers.
3. Talk to school principals, counselors, or others.
4. Talk to family members such as parents, grandparents, and siblings.
5. Talk to friends.

are in a bad mood and whether teasing gets on their nerves. Sometimes, overweight or obese students let the teaser know that he or she has crossed the line and it hurts their feelings. Very often, the teaser will just back off. Sometimes, overweight or obese students use verbal confrontations by lashing out, "checking," or teasing the teaser. Overweight or obese students might check the teaser by talking badly about his or her hair or clothing. Sometimes, overweight or obese students get into physical confrontations with the teaser. In other situations, overweight or obese students confront the teaser by challenging him or her in the physical activities or sports about which they are teased. Overweight or obese students try to prove the teaser wrong. For example, during a relay race, a thin student teased an overweight student, saying, "You cannot do it." This overweight student proved this thin student wrong by racing and beating him (Li et al., 2012).

Stress Reduction

According to the Transactional Model (Lazarus & Folkman, 1984), stress occurs when external pressures exceed a person's ability to handle them. Stress is not a direct response to a stressful event. It is a result of one's level of resources to cope with stressful events in his or her life. Stress can negatively impact students' health outcomes. The ways that students cope with stress can reduce the negative impact of stress on their health outcomes. Overweight or obese students experience a lot of stress as a result of obesity bias or weight-related teasing. Thus the strategies that overweight or obese students use to cope with stress are critical in alleviating its negative effects on their psychosocial, health, and emotional well-being.

The previously mentioned studies showed that overweight or obese students have successfully used a variety of stress-reduction strategies to cope with obesity bias or weight-related teasing in physical education classes. Some coping strategies can be beneficial to overweight or obese students by preventing them from emotional distress or by enabling them to recovery quickly from emotional distress. They focused themselves on their interests or enjoyable activities such as listening to music, reading a book, going shopping, working on model cars, and so forth. For example, one overweight or obese student shared, "I used to go to Wal-Mart and buy me little model cars and stuff, go in my room, sit in there and just put them together all at one time, it used to release stress off my mind." On the other hand, many other coping strategies can be detrimental to over-weight or obese students' psychosocial, emotional, and behav-ioral well-being. Overweight or obese students use binge eating, taking drugs, suicide attempts, isolating themselves from their peers and family members, and injuring themselves to release themselves from the distress caused by teasing. For example, one overweight or obese student commented,

> I remember one time. I was real mad. Somebody checked me really bad. I would go home and start choking myself. I was trying to kill myself because I did not want to be here. I thought I was not going to be nothing in life. I did not want to be here because I did not think anybody would ever like me. That is why I tried to kill myself. I would stab, cut, or stick myself to take the pain away from me.

Another overweight or obese student used binge eating to relieve himself from the negative effects of teasing. This student reported, "When I'm sad, I tend to eat more. I guess a lot of the time I've been sad, like I suffer from depression. When I get depressed, I'll just eat, eat, eat, eat, and that's how I got big then."

Physical education teachers should be knowledgeable about these adaptive and maladaptive stress-reduction coping strate-gies, and then educate overweight or obese students to adopt these adaptive strategies to relieve stress from being teased.

A number of adaptive and maladaptive strategies are presented in Table 3.3 so that physical education teachers can share them with their students. This list can be posted on the bulletin board inside the gymnasium or handed out to students. It can also be sent home to students' parents in the form of a brochure or newsletter so that they can incorporate coping tools to help their children to recover quickly from stress.

Self-Protection

Overweight or obese students use self-protection as a mechanism to cope against weight-related teasing (for an in-depth

Table 3.3 Adaptive and Maladaptive Stress-Reduction Coping Strategies Used by Overweight or Obese Students

Adaptive coping strategies	Maladaptive coping strategies
1. Build model cars.	1. Engage in binge eating.
2. Go shopping.	2. Take drugs.
3. Make key chains.	3. Physically hurt yourself.
4. Listen to music.	4. Attempt suicide.
5. Get on a dance team.	5. Stop talking to other people.
6. Get a pencil and paper to draw or write things.	6. Sleep.
7. Play sports such as tennis or swimming.	7. Isolate yourself after school.
8. Write a poem to express yourself as a sweet, intelligent, sensitive, smart, determined, quiet, respectful girl or boy.	
9. Write about your bad feelings and negative experience in journals.	
10. Go for a walk.	
11. Read a book.	

review, see Li & Rukavina, 2009; Puhl & Brownell, 2003). Using this mechanism, overweight or obese students can attribute negative outcomes to other people's feelings of insecurity or prejudiced attitudes rather than their own personal ability and attributes; contrast themselves to other students who are worse off to feel better; avoid showing incompetence in themselves; enhance their receptivity by valuing their gifted areas; and engage in positive self-talks. Li, Rukavina, and Wright (2012) found that overweight or obese students perceived teasing/bias as other students' problem and did not attribute it to lack of ability in themselves. These participants also believed that the teaser must feel really bad about him/herself, had a problem with him/herself, was simply crazy, or had low self-esteem issues. They raised their self-esteem by positive self-talk such as reassuring themselves that they have the skills and ability to do things, having a good personality, focusing on the inside (big heart, caring) rather than the size of their body, and valuing the sports that they are good at. These self-protective coping strategies have great potential to help overweight or obese students protect and raise their self-esteem or confidence levels. For example, Myers and Rosen's (1999) study found that strategies such as positive self-talk and viewing situations as the other's issue or problem are positively associated with high levels of self-esteem.

Compensation

Compensation is another mechanism that overweight or obese students use to cope with obesity bias or weight-related teasing (for an in-depth review, see Li & Rukavina, 2009; Puhl & Brownell, 2003). Compensation means that one makes up for a weakness in one area by gaining strength in another area. Overweight or obese students try to work hard to get better at sports and games so that others can change their perceptions of them. They use words such as "try to do better," "never give up," "keep trying," "work hard at it," and "push yourself" to describe their effort. Overweight or obese students try to increase their lik-ability by responding positively, being friendly and nice, being good natured, sharing items of interest, trying to fit in the group, or making a lot of funny jokes. For example, one overweight or obese student made fun of his own weight, which allowed him to make friends with his peers and diffuse any jokes coming at him (Li et al., 2012).

Losing Weight

To escape from being teased, overweight or obese students try to lose body weight (Li et al., 2012; Neumark-Sztainer et al., 1998; Puhl & Brownell, 2006). They may go on a diet, try not to over-eat junk food, and try to participate in physical activities. Oth-ers try to eat healthier meals and exercise more to become fit. For example, one overweight or obese student reported, "I try to eat right and exercise most of the time. I do things that are right for me." The etiologies of obesity are complex and multi-faceted. Most weight-loss experiences have not been successful. If overweight or obese students' weight-loss attempts are not successful, it can lead to further self-blame for being the object of other people's bias or stigmatized beliefs. Therefore, physical education teachers should educate all students to develop and maintain a healthy, physically active lifestyle.

Use of Multiple Coping Strategies under Different Mechanisms

As reported by Li et al. (2012), overweight or obese students used multiple strategies under different coping mechanisms to deal with obesity bias. The use of these coping strategies often progresses as the teasing event develops. If overweight or obese students are not bothered by the teasing, they will ignore it and walk away. However, when the teasing gets serious and begins to hurt overweight or obese students' feelings, they may verbally or physically confront the teaser (Li et al., 2012). For example, one overweight or obese student employed multiple coping strategies under three different mechanisms—avoidance, stress reduction, and confrontation—to deal with weight-related teasing. This student commented,

> Sometimes the boys will start checking me, and I'll tell them . . . I'll tell them to stop, but they don't stop. So I just go away from them and leave it alone. I'll just be quiet. Sometimes, when I'm quiet, I'll read. I'll hide behind my book and cry and stuff like that.
>
> (Li et al., 2012, p. 193)

Following is a summary of coping strategies that physical education teachers can provide to overweight or obese students who can then strategically select them to cope with weight-related teasing.

- Try your best to ignore the teasing.
- Do not pay attention to the teasers' negative comments; brush them off, let them go past your body, look over them, or do not listen to them.
- Talk to the teasers and tell them how you feel.
- Laugh in the teaser's face after hearing the negative comment.
- Avoid the teasing by minding your own business or just doing the things you do.
- Do the things you are good at to make yourself feel good.
- Do not care about what your peers think about you.
- Do not take the teasing seriously.
- When you are being teased, turn around and talk to your friends; pretend that you do not hear the teaser.
- When others start teasing or checking each other, stay out of the conversation.

- Avoid the teasers whenever possible.
- Change the subject, start a new conversation, or walk away when others start teasing or checking you.
- Confront the teaser by saying that that is not OK and he or she has crossed the line.
- Prove the teasers wrong if you can.
- Challenge the teasers to a contest or dare the teasers to do it themselves.
- When you are teased by others, try to find a fault in them and bring it to their awareness, or let them know that everyone has their own areas of strengths and weaknesses.
- Confront the teaser by making a joke back to them.
- Have good social skills, be humorous and good natured, and make friends.
- Be around friendly and supportive peers to avoid the teasers.
- Create a network of friends who will stand up for you if somebody tries to tease you.
- Deal with the teasing by telling a teacher or an adult.
- Always think positively about yourself.
- Use stress or relaxation strategies to cope with the negative emotions that result from being teased.
- Cry it out.
- Talk to someone for support after being teased.
- Get your mind off of the teasing or relieve stress by working on building projects like Legos or model cars, joining a dance team, reading a book, listening to music, making key chains, coloring designs and drawing, writing out emotions, and playing sports.
- Use religion to help you accept yourself.
- Think that the teasers are crazy or have low self-esteem to make the teasing not hurt you.

- Use positive self-talk to deal with the emotions that result from teasing.
- Sweat it off by dancing or exercising to music or sleep off the negative emotions.
- Lose body weight by exercising more and eating healthier meals.
- Keep holding on and believing in yourself that you can do as well as others in sports.
- Actively participate in physical education and do the best you can do.
- Keep trying and never give up in physical education classes.
- Be yourself and have confidence in yourself in physical education.
- Focus positively on yourself. What matters is the inside (your mind and heart), not the outside or how you look.
- Diffuse teasing by trying to get along with others even if they are mean to you.
- Be proud of who you are, and do not feel down about yourself.

Choices of Coping Strategy Depends on the Situation and Its Effectiveness as Learned through Trial and Error

Not all coping strategies can be effective for overweight or obese students to deal with obesity bias. Some strategies might work in certain situations but not in others. Some strategies might work for some overweight or obese students but not for other students. The use of coping strategies is shaped by the specific context in which teasing occurs (Folkman et al., 1986; Lazarus & Folkman, 1984). The findings from Li and colleagues' (2012) study showed that determining which coping strategies to use is dependent on the situation in which obesity bias occurs. Overweight or obese students reported numerous reasons for their choice of coping strategies, including whether they wanted to fight at that moment, how confident they felt about themselves, where they were being teased, and who was teasing them (Li et al., 2012). Very often, if the teasing did not bother overweight or obese students, they would just ignore it and walk away. For example, one overweight or obese student in Li et al.'s (2012) study reported,

> Well, when I just got sick of it, I would just be like . . . ignore it, and they won't have anything else to say because they would just ignore it or either sometimes my classmates . . . they will lash back . . . but sometimes I know that they are playing with me and I know that I'm playing with them so it's just like okay, and we're just playing and sometimes they really mean it and I have to go back and lash out at them . . . but sometimes I just ignore it because I know they are playing with me.
>
> (p. 194)

The effectiveness of a coping strategy is normally discovered through trial and error (Li et al., 2012). When one strategy does not work, overweight or obese students will try to use another coping strategy. For example, in Li et al.'s (2012) study, one overweight or obese student confronted the teasers by telling them to stop. When this coping strategy did not work, this overweight or obese student walked away from the teasers and left it alone. The student shared,

> Sometimes the boys will start checking me, and I'll tell them . . . and I'll tell them to stop, but they don't stop. So I just go away from them and leave it alone. I'll just be quiet.
>
> (p. 193)

Parental Support for Students When They Are Teased

Parents play a critical role in affecting how their children cope with stressful events (Contreras et al., 2000; Kliewer, Fearnow, & Miller, 1996; Kliewer, Fearnow, & Walton, 1998). They can directly alleviate the negative effects of stress by talking to their children, or indirectly provide specific strategies for their children to deal with stressors (Beehr & McGrath, 1992; Lakey & Cohen, 2000). Parental support can also protect overweight or obese students from the suffering of various forms of bullying (Wang, Iannotti, & Nansel, 2009). Prior studies have shown that overweight or obese students preferred support intervention from their parents (Puhl, Peterson, & Luedicke, 2013), and actively sought support and advice from their parents to cope with the negative effects as a result of being teased at school (Li et al., 2012). In some cases, overweight or obese students just wanted to have a conversation with their parents about the negative experience so that they could vent their negative emotions. In other cases, they actively asked parents to give them advice on how to cope with teasing (Li et al., 2012).

Given the critical role parents play in helping their children cope with obesity bias and in protecting them from the psychological and emotional damage that results from being teased in PE, it is very important to equip parents with their own coping strategies. Knowledge of these strategies can help parents better educate their overweight or obese children about how to deal with teasing and thus reduce or shield themselves from its negative effects. The following list contains a number of coping strategies and support that physical education teachers can provide to their students' parents, thus helping them better handle the situation when their child is teased at school (Li & Rukavina, unpublished manuscript). These strategies range from just listening carefully to the children talk, getting involved by talking to the teasers' parents or school principals, seeking support from other professionals, to physically removing the bully by changing classes or even schools.

- Communicate to your child that you love and care about him.
- Be connected to your child and engage in a conversation with her as friends. Talk about things that are important to her and how she feels and what is going on in her life.
- Be there to support your child by listening, talking to him, and showing understanding.
- Encourage your child to adopt healthier eating patterns, and get involved by exercising with her.
- To develop your child's self-esteem and motivation, focus on his positive aspects instead of his weight.
- Be a role model. Parents can set a good example when the whole family does it. For example, instead of telling your child to go out and ride her bicycle, the family can all go out biking together.
- Be aware of the environments where teasing is taking place. If your child is frequently teased in Mr. Perry's class and the teasing becomes too demeaning or stressful for him or her, then you can move your child out of that environment by switching him or her to another classroom.
- Have a physician check out what causes your child's weight gain besides food intake.
- Education is the key; try to instill the concept of being healthy.
- Sit down and talk to adolescents and let them know that they have to cope together by dieting and exercising together.
- Let your child know that you are not ashamed of her.

- Change family dieting and exercise habits. Make the child understand that you love him, and you are doing this because you want him to live long, be healthy, and be prosperous.
- Positively communicate the teasing issue to the parents of the teaser or bully.
- Go to the school and talk to the teacher and principal in person.
- Have God in your life. Your child can pray when he or she feels left out or is teased by peers at school. Praying to God may help your child reduce anger and stress and feel better.
- Teach your child about nutrition and making good choices while grocery shopping.
- Use positive reinforcements.
- Find some professional groups for help.
- Advise your child to talk to a close friend.
- Monitor child's food intake and watch her proportion sizes. Do not let your child fix her own plate.
- Teach your child to think positive thoughts, not negative or revengeful thoughts.
- Tell your child to say no to junk food such as hamburgers, pizza, and french fries.
- Discuss teasing with your child, and tell him to walk away from the teasers.
- Tell your child to be happy with what God has given to her, whether looks or talents.
- Seek support from other parents who are dealing with the same issues.
- Organize opportunities for your child to work out in the school gym.
- Be supportive of other healthy choices for your child such as enrolling him or her in after-school sports or physical activity programs or buying fruits and vegetables.

- Use the Internet to look up information or research for better education on how to exercise scientifically and eat healthy food.
- Teach your child that only he can change himself.
- Check to make sure that there is nothing wrong with your child first, and then feed her properly and have the right foods in the house.
- Go to support groups.
- Explain to your child that everyone has a different body weight.
- Go to a counselor if you do not know how to help.
- Cut back on the greasy foods and cut off television and video game time at home.
- Try to keep your child positive. Do not let him think that it is his problem and he is the cause of it.
- Work with your child and do not let her feel that she is alone or that she is in it by herself.
- Be connected with schools and know what your child is doing there.
- When your child will not listen to you, try to get other family or community members to talk to him.
- Be careful and sensitive of how you talk to your child. Do not call your child names. Try to tell her something to pick her spirit up. Tell her something funny about your day.
- Let your child make his own decisions to lose weight. Do not force him to do it.
- Have your child on a budget, and do not give her too much extra money.
- Do not say anything negative to your child about his weight.
- Do not punish your child for being overweight or obese.
- Do not tell your child that she is fat and nobody is going to like her.

- If your child is overweight, do not assume it is because he is lazy and does not want to exercise.
- Do not put fuel in the fire by attacking and depressing your child even more. Try to understand; sit your child down, talk and listen to her, and try to help her through the situation.
- Physically separate the bully from your child by changing your child's class or by enrolling him at a different school (Puhl et al., 2013).
- Enroll your child in a new group or community program where she can make new friends (Puhl et al., 2013).

Summary

This chapter discussed the definition of coping and overweight or obese students' coping mechanisms and strategies. Specific strategies for overweight or obese students and their parents are provided. Physical education teachers can include these specific strategies in their weekly newsletter to parents. A list of teaching strategies that can potentially reduce obesity bias are provided for physical education teachers. Instructors need to recognize that some of these strategies are developed based on research evidence supporting their effectiveness, while others are developed based on little or no research evidence supporting their effectiveness. Even though there may be minimal research evidence, these teaching strategies can still work effectively to reduce obesity bias among students.

References

Barrera, M., Jr. (1986). Distinctions between social support concepts, measures, and models. *American Journal of Community Psychology, 14,* 413–445.

Beehr, T. A., & McGrath, J. E. (1992). Social support, occupational stress, and anxiety. *Anxiety, Stress, and Coping, 5,* 7–19.

Contreras, J. M., Kerns, K. A., Weimer, B. L., Gentzler, A. L., & Tomich, P. L. (2000). Emotion regulation as mediator of associations between mother-child attachment and peer relationships in middle childhood. *Journal of Family Psychology, 14*, 111–124.

Eisenberg, M. E., Neumark-Sztainer, D., Haines, J., & Wall, M. (2006). Weight teasing and emotional well-being in adolescents: Longitudinal findings from project EAT. *Journal of Adolescent Health, 28*, 675–683.

Faith, M. S., Leone, M. A., Ayer, T. S., Heo, M., & Pietrobelli, A. (2002). Weight criticism during physical activity, coping skills, and reported physical activity in children. *Pediatrics, 110*, e23.

Folkman, S., Lazarus, R. S., Dunkel-Schetter, C., DeLongis, A., & Gruen, R. J. (1986). Dynamics of a stressful encounter: Cognitive appraisal, coping, and encounter outcomes. *Journal of Personality and Social Psychology, 50*, 992–1003.

Kliewer, W., Fearnow, M. D., & Miller, P. A. (1996). Coping socialization in middle childhood: Tests of maternal and paternal influences. *Child Development, 67*, 2339–2357.

Kliewer, W., Fearnow, M. D., & Walton, M. N. (1998). Dispositional, environmental, and context-specific predictors of children's threat of perceptions in everyday stressful situations. *Journal of Youth and Adolescence, 27*, 83–100.

Lakey, B., & Cohen, S. (2000). Social support theory and selecting measures of social support. In S. Cohen, L. U. Gordon, & B. H. Gottlieb (Eds.), *Social support measurement and interventions: A guide for health and social scientists* (pp. 29–52). New York: Oxford University Press.

Lakey, B., & Drew, J. B. (1997). A social-cognitive perspective on social support. In G. R. Pierce, B. Lakey, I. G. Sarason, & B. R. Sarason (Eds.), *Source book of social support and personality* (pp. 107–140). New York: Plenum.

Lazarus, R. S., & Folkman, S. (1984). *Stress, appraisal, and coping*. New York: Springer.

Li, W., & Rukavina, P. (2009). A review on coping mechanisms against obesity bias in physical activity/education settings. *Obesity Reviews, 10*, 87–95.

Li, W., & Rukavina, P. (2012). The nature, occurring contexts, and psychological implications of weight-related teasing in urban physical education programs. *Research Quarterly for Exercise and Sport, 83*(2), 308–317.

Li, W., & Rukavina, P. (unpublished manuscript). *Types and nature of parental support for overweight students to cope with weight-related teasing.*

Li, W., Rukavina, P., & Wright, P. (2012). Coping against weight-related teasing among adolescents perceived to be overweight or obese in urban physical education. *Journal of Teaching in Physical Education, 31*, 182–199.

Mellin, A. E., Neumark-Sztainer, D., Story, M., Ireland, M., & Resnick, M. D. (2002). Unhealthy behaviors and psychosocial difficulties among overweight adolescents: The potential impact of familial factors. *Journal of Adolescent Health, 31*, 145–153.

Myers, A., & Rosen, J. C. (1999). Obesity stigmatization and coping: Relation to mental health symptoms, body image, and self-esteem. *International Journal of Obesity, 23*, 221–230.

Neumark-Sztainer, D., Story, M., & Faibisch, L. (1998). Perceived stigmatization among overweight African-American and Caucasian adolescent girls. *Journal of Adolescent Health, 23*, 264–270.

Parker, J. D., & Endler, N. S. (1992). Coping with coping assessment: A critical review. *European Journal of Personality, 6*, 321–344.

Pierce, G. R., Sarason, I. G., & Sarason, B. R. (1996). Coping and social support. In M. Zeidner, & N. S. Endler (Eds.), *Handbook of coping: Theory, research, application* (pp. 434–451). New York: John Wiley & Sons.

Puhl, R. M., & Brownell, K. D. (2003). Ways of coping with obesity stigma: Review and conceptual analysis. *Eating Behaviors, 4*, 53–78.

Puhl, R. M., & Brownell, K. D. (2006). Confronting and coping with weight stigma: An investigation of overweight and obese adults. *Obesity, 10*, 1802–1815.

Puhl, R. M., Peterson, J. L., & Luedicke, J. (2013). Strategies to address weight-based victimization: Youths' preferred support interventions from classmates, teachers, and parents. *Journal of Youth and Adolescence, 42*, 315–327.

Wang, J., Iannotti, R. J., & Nansel, T. R. (2009). School bullying among adolescents in the United States: Physical, verbal, relational and cyber. *Journal of Adolescent Health, 45*, 368–375.

4

A CONCEPTUAL FRAMEWORK FOR INCLUSION
SOCIAL ECOLOGICAL CONSTRAINT MODEL

As discussed in the previous chapters, obesity among children and adolescents has increased at an alarming rate. Obesity is not only associated with many cardiovascular and heart diseases (Physical Activity Guidelines Advisory Committee, 2008), but also has serious psychosocial and emotional consequences (Li & Rukavina, 2012b; Storch et al., 2007). Due to their body weight, overweight or obese students in general have lower physical ability, skills, and fitness as compared to their normal-weight peers (Dumith et al., 2010; Okely, Booth, & Chey, 2004). In addition, overweight or obese children and youth are often stigmatized as being unmotivated, less intelligent, less attractive, or less athletic by peers at school (Puhl & Latner, 2007; Zeller, Reiter-Purtill, & Ramey,

2008), and are commonly teased or even excluded from participating in physical education (Curtis, 2008; Fox & Edmunds, 2000; Li & Rukavina, 2012b; Trout & Graber, 2009).

Weight-related teasing is associated with psychological and emotional damage in children (Li & Rukavina, 2012b; Storch et al., 2007) and can lead overweight students to not enjoy physical activity (Faith et al., 2002) or be unsatisfied with their PE lessons (Kamtsios & Digelidis, 2008). The widespread obesity issue and its associated health and psychosocial consequences have presented an unprecedented challenge for PE teachers to create an inclusive classroom for overweight or obese students to be actively engaged in PE. There is an urgent need to equip PE instructors with a conceptual model and specific teaching strategies so that they can design appropriate curricular content and instruction. This would allow them to create positive, inclusive learning environments to successfully involve overweight or obese students in physical education activities.

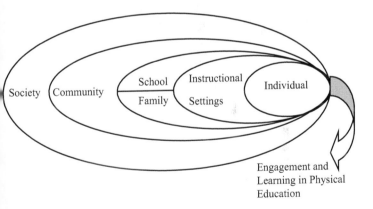

Figure 4.1 Social Ecological Constraint Model for Inclusion of Overweight Students into Physical Education

Source: Li, W. & Rukavina, P. (2012a). Including overweight or obese students in physical education: A social ecological constraint model. *Research Quarterly for Exercise and Sports, 83*, 570–578(9). Copyrights Permission Granted.

This chapter presents the Social Ecological Constraint Model (Li & Rukavina, 2012a) as reflected in Figure 4.1. We will define constraints and discuss various constraints at each of five levels— individual overweight students, instructional settings, school/ family, community, and society. Specific examples are provided to help physical education teachers understand these constraints and their effect on overweight or obese students' engagement and learning in physical education. As an agent of change, physical education instructors should recognize various constraints at different levels, and strategically manipulate these modifiable constraints for effective inclusion of overweight students in PE.

What Is Constraint?

Obesity is commonly associated with negativity. This negativity has had a serious effect on overweight or obese students' psychosocial, emotional, and behavioral outcomes. Therefore, it is critical to conceptualize the notion of being overweight or obese as constraints in a more inclusive way in relation to the individual's situation (Gagen & Getchell, 2006; Getchell & Gagen, 2006). Constraint is a neutral term, which can refer to any factors that either facilitate/afford or inhibit students' movement patterns or behaviors relative to the situations (Newell, 1986). For example, peer support is a constraint that can motivate overweight or obese students to become more engaged in PE in every situation. Body weight is another constraint, and its effect on overweight or obese students' behaviors is dependent on the situations. It can facilitate overweight or obese students' performance, for example, when they play offensive/defensive lineman in football. However, when overweight or obese students run for a mile, body weight can inhibit their performance (Li & Rukavina, 2012a).

Social Ecological Constraint Model

Overweight or obese students' engagement and behaviors in physical education classes can be influenced by numerous constraints, which include school and community physical environments, school cultures, peer interactions, characteristics of individual students, instructional tasks, class rules, parental attitudes and behaviors, community cultures and resources, societal cultures, beliefs and expectations, policies, and legislation. Inclusion of overweight or obese students in PE is complex and multifaceted, as opposed to just modifying equipment and activities or empowering overweight or obese students with activity choices. Recently, Li and Rukavina (2012a) have proposed a Social Ecological Constraint Model to study the issue of inclusion of overweight or obese students in physical education. Teachers, as an agent of change, must first recognize various constraints occurring at different levels, and then strategically manipulate these particular modifiable constraints at different levels to include overweight or obese students in PE (Li & Rukavina, 2012a).

According to the Social Ecological Constraint Model, there are numerous constraints existing on five levels of the ecology, which can have an impact on overweight or obese students' learning and behaviors in PE. As reflected in Figure 4.1, the five levels consist of individuals, PE instructional settings, school/family, community, and society. Physical education instructors are change agents who can manipulate various constraints at the five levels for effective inclusion of overweight students in their classes (Li & Rukavina, 2012a).

Numerous constraints at the individual level can influence the inclusion of overweight or obese students in physical education (Li & Rukavina, 2012a). They include body weight and height, sports ability and skill level, self-efficacy, self-perception, motivation, stereotypical beliefs and biases, attitudes, social economic class, gender, race/ethnicity, and interests. These individual constraints can be sorted into two categories—structural and functional (Li & Rukavina, 2012a). Structural constraints are associated with specific body structures such as body weight, body height, or muscle strength. Functional constraints refer to specific functions of the body structure. They consist of attitudes, ability beliefs, motivation, gender and racial stereotypical beliefs, cognition, emotion, weight stigma and bias, and socioeconomic class.

Excessive body weight as a structural constraint can negatively influence overweight or obese students' performance in certain activities and sports in PE such as fitness activities. They may not be able to run as fast, or do as many push-ups and sit-ups as their normal-weight peers. However, body weight can benefit overweight or obese students' performance when playing a defensive or offensive linemen position in football (Li & Rukavina, 2012a; Li, Li, Zhao, & Li, in press).

Another individual constraint is an overweight or obese student's skill and ability levels. As compared to their normal-weight peers, overweight or obese students generally have lower skills and abilities (Dumith et al., 2010; Okely et al., 2004). They tend to not perform as well as their peers in many sports and fitness activities such as soccer, basketball, running, sit-ups, jumping rope, or push-ups.

Our society holds obesity bias toward overweight or obese individuals. However, overweight or obese students can become self-motivated to become engaged in sports and physical activities to resist obesity bias and change societal bias. On the other hand, obesity bias can negatively affect overweight or obese students' emotions, motivation, and behaviors, especially when they internalize obesity bias (Hilbert, Braehler, Haeuser, & Zenger, 2014). Research has demonstrated that overweight or obese individuals who internalize obesity bias display more frequent binge eating, refuse to diet, and report lower core self-evaluation in response to obesity bias (Puhl & Latner, 2007; Hilbert et al., 2014).

Overweight or obese students are often self-conscious of their body weight (Li & Rukavian, 2012b). As another individual constraint, self-consciousness of body weight can sometimes be a motivator for overweight or obese students to modify their lifestyle behaviors. To change their body image, overweight or obese students begin to eat healthier and do more exercises. However, self-consciousness of body weight often has a negative effect on overweight or obese students' engagement and learning in physical education (Li & Rukavian, 2012b). Due to being self-conscious of their body weight, overweight or obese students are often embarrassed to change clothes in the locker room in front of their peers, and perceive themselves as being inferior to their peers with regard to sports skills and physical abilities (Li & Rukavian, 2012b).

Other individual constraints are self-efficacy/self-confidence and motivation. Self-confidence/self-efficacy and motivation are significant predictors of students' engagement and behaviors in physical education (Gao, Lochbaum, & Podlog, 2011; Gao, Xiang, Lochbaum, & Guan, 2013; Guan, Xiang, McBride, & Keating, 2013; Li, Lee, & Solmon, 2005; Slingerland, Haerens, Cardon, & Borghouts, 2014; Xiang, McBride, Bruene, & Liu, 2007). Overweight or obese students often lack confidence and motivation to become engaged in physical education. Due to lack of confidence and motivation, overweight or obese students often try to avoid showing deficiency in skills or abilities in physical education classes by sitting on the bleachers or putting minimal effort into group activities.

The PE instructional settings level includes constraints occurring in an instructional setting. Examples of constraints in PE instructional settings include learning the task, physical environments, and social climates. The physical and social environmental constraints include space, lights, learning climates, facilities, peer interactions, student-teacher interactions, and equipment. The type of teaching philosophy that an instructor adopts can affect overweight or obese students' engagement and learning in physical education. Thus, overweight or obese students can benefit more from an inclusive teaching philosophy, whereas instructors focus on teaching all students equitably. This can be provided by using differentiated instruction to students with different skills and ability levels and by creating inclusive, motivating, caring learning climates. The types of unit goals and contents, fitness tests and score reports, feedback, game rules, space, equipment and facilities, instructional models or methods, and managerial and organizational skills are other examples of constraints at the instructional setting that can affect overweight students' engagement and learning in physical education. In a positive, caring learning environment, overweight or obese students can become motivated to engage in learning in physical education. In an equitable and caring environment, students are more willing to persist longer and put in more effort in the face of difficulties. As a result, overweight or obese students can improve their skills and performance. In contrast, in a negative learning environment where teachers focus on social comparisons and superiority, overweight or obese students will be discouraged about engaging in physical education. They will give up easily when facing difficulties and challenges and put forth little or no effort, which will result in performance deterioration.

The school and family level consists of constraints existing in school and at home, including school policies and rules, school culture and values, parent–teacher associations, school physical environments, classroom teachers and administrators, home environments, parental attitudes and behaviors, child–parent relationships, and siblings and peers. For example, in a family oriented school where people treat one another with respect and kindness, overweight students will feel they are being included and will experience less teasing. In schools where parent–teacher associations are actively hosting programs and events, overweight students will have better opportunities and access to sports and physical activities and will be better able to develop and maintain a healthy, physically active lifestyle. Parents' attitudes toward healthy eating, exercise, and lifestyle behaviors play a significant role in shaping their children's attitudes toward healthy eating, exercise, and lifestyle behaviors. In general, children whose parents live a healthy, physically active lifestyle are more likely to adopt a healthy, physical active lifestyle themselves. Children whose parents live a sedentary lifestyle are more likely to be sedentary as well.

The community level includes constraints with regard to community cultures and values, community organizations, churches, community programs and resources, exercise clubs, community sport leagues, and neighborhood built-in environments such as playgrounds, swimming pools, walking trails, and recreational centers. The more affluent the community, the better the resources provided for the community to live a healthy, physically active lifestyle. Overweight students whose family live in a community where playgrounds with equipment and facilities and walking and biking trails are available are more likely to be engaged in sports and physical activity outside school. Overweight students whose families live in a poor, unsafe community are more likely to live a sedentary lifestyle (watching television and playing video games) outside school.

Constraints at the societal level are composed of legislation, guidelines and policies, social and cultural norms, stereotypical beliefs (i.e., stigma, bias, gender, and race stereotypes), and discriminations. Numerous national physical activity and public health guidelines, documents, and initiatives have been published in response to the dramatic increase in obesity among children and adults in the past decade (Li et al., 2016). These national guidelines, documents, and initiatives have called upon schools' physical education programs to provide more opportunities for children to engage in moderate to vigorous physical activity. This urgent call has provided physical activity in a more friendly environment, where overweight or obese students can have greater opportunities to be physically active. On the other hand, obesity bias/weight stigma is another constraint, which can negatively impact overweight or obese students' engagement and learning in PE. Because of body weight, overweight or obese students often experience prejudice by their peers toward their sport skills and ability. They are often perceived as having inferior sports abilities and skills than their slimmer peers. As a result, overweight students are often the last to be chosen for a team simply because their peers with normal weight believe that they are not good at what they do (Doolittle et al., 2016; Rukavina et al., 2015).

Summary

The Social Ecological Constraint Model provides physical education teachers with a viable conceptual framework to successfully include overweight or obese students in their program. Physical education instructors must situate their program within this social ecology, recognize various constraints at different levels, and then strategically manipulate these constraints to include overweight or obese students through differentiated instruction and a caring learning environment. Some constraints can be easily modified to meet the needs of overweight or obese students, such as equipment and instruction. Others may be more difficult to modify such as weight stigma and criticism, stereotypical beliefs, and policies. Stigma and stereotypical beliefs are deeply ingrained in the mind-sets of individuals in our society. A whole-school approach over a longer period of time will be required to make any significant changes. When physical education teachers take actions to reduce stigma and stereotypical beliefs, they should expect to encounter significant resistance. Various constraints at different levels affect one another. A change in one constraint at one level will affect changes in other constraints at the same level or different levels. Therefore, physical education instructors should focus on manipulating constraints not only at the instructional levels, but also at other levels to successfully provide an inclusive learning environment for overweight or obese students.

References

Curtis, P. (2008). The experiences of young people with obesity in secondary school: Some implications for the healthy school agenda. *Health and Social Care in the Community, 16*, 410–418.

Doolittle, S., Rukavina, P., Li, W., Manson, M., & Beale, A. (2016). Middle school physical education teachers' perspectives on overweight students. *Journal of Teaching in Physical Education, 35*, 127–137.

Dumith, S. C., Ramires, W., Souza, M. A., Moraes, D. S., Petry, F. G., Oliveira, E. S., . . . Hallal P. C. (2010). Overweight/obesity and physical fitness among children and adolescents. *Journal of Physical Activity and Health, 7*, 641–648.

Faith, M. S., Leone, M. A., Ayers, T. S., Heo, M., & Pietrobelli, A. (2002). Weight criticism during physical activity, coping skills, and reported physical activity in children. *Pediatrics, 110*, e23.

Fox, K. R., & Edmunds, L. D. (2000). Understanding the world of the "fat kid": Schools help provide a better experience? *Reclaiming Child Youth: Journal of Emotion Behavior Problems, 9*, 177–181.

Gagen, L., & Getchell, N. (2006). Using "constraints" to design developmentally appropriate movement activities for early childhood education. *Early Childhood Education Journal, 34*, 227–232.

Gao, Z., Lochbaum, M., & Podlog, L. (2011). Self-efficacy as a mediator of children's achievement motivation and in-class physical activity. *Perceptual and Motor Skills, 113*, 969–981.

Gao, Z., Xiang, P., Lochbaum, M., & Guan, J. (2013). The impact of achievement goals on cardiorespiratory fitness: Does self-efficacy make a difference? *Research Quarterly for Exercise and Sport, 84*, 313–322.

Getchell, N., & Gagen, L. (2006). Adapting activities for all children: Considering constraints can make planning simple and effective. *Palaestra, 22,* 20–27, 43, 58.

Guan, J., Xiang, P., McBride, R., & Keating, X. D. (2013). Achievement goals, social goals, and students' reported persistence and effort in high school athletic settings. *Journal of Sport Behavior, 36,* 149–170.

Hilbert, A., Braehler, E., Haeuser, W., & Zenger, M. (2014). Weight bias internalization, core self-evaluation, and health in overweight and obese persons. *Obesity, 22,* 79–85.

Kamtsios, S., & Digelidis, N. (2008). Physical activity levels, exercise attitudes, self-perceptions and BMI type of 11 to 12-year-old children. *Journal of Child Health Care, 12,* 232–240.

Li, H., Li, W., Zhao, Q., & Li, M. (in press). Including overweight or obese students in physical education: An urgent need and effective teaching strategies. *Journal of Physical Education, Recreation and Dance.*

Li, W., Lee, A. M., & Solmon, M. A. (2005). Relationship among dispositional ability conceptions, intrinsic motivation, perceived competence, experience, and performance. *Journal of Teaching in Physical Education, 24,* 51–65.

Li, W., & Rukavina, P. (2012a). Including overweight or obese students in physical education: A social ecological constraint model. *Research Quarterly for Exercise and Sports, 83,* 570–578.

Li, W., & Rukavina, P. (2012b). The nature, occurring contexts, and psychological implications of weight-related teasing in urban physical education programs. *Research Quarterly for Exercise and Sport, 83,* 308–317.

Li, W., Xiang, P., Gao, Z., Shen, B., Yin, Z., & Kong, Q. (2016). Impact of national physical activity and health guidelines and documents on research on teaching K–12 physical education in U.S.A. *Journal of Teaching in Physical Education, 35,* 85–96.

Newell, K. M. (1986). Constraint on the development of coordination. In M. Wade & H. T. A. Whiting (Eds.), *Motor development in children: Aspects of coordination and control* (pp. 341–360). Dordecht, The Netherlands: Martinus Nijholf.

Okely, A. D., Booth, M. L., & Chey, T. (2004). Relationships between body composition and fundamental movement skills among children and adolescents. *Research Quarterly for Exercise and Sport, 75,* 238–247.

Physical Activity Guidelines Advisory Committee. (2008). *Physical activity guidelines advisory committee report.* Washington, DC: U.S. Department of Health and Human Services.

Puhl, R., & Latner, J. D. (2007). Stigma, obesity, and the health of the nation's children. *Psychological Bulletin, 133,* 557–580.

Rukavina, P. B., Doolittle, S., Li, W., Manson, M., & Beale, A. (2015). Middle school teachers' strategies for including overweight students in skill and fitness instruction. *Journal of Teaching in Physical Education, 34*, 93–118. doi: 10.1123/jtpe.2013–0152

Slingerland, M., Haerens, L., Cardon, G., & Borghouts, L. (2014). Differences in perceived competence and physical activity levels during single-gender modified basketball game play in middle school physical education. *European Physical Education Review, 20*, 20–35. doi: 10.1177/1356336X13496000

Storch, E. A., Milsom, V. A., DeBraganza, N., Lewin, A. B., Geffken, G. R., & Silverstein, J. H. (2007). Peer victimization, psychosocial adjustment, and physical activity in overweight and at-risk-for-overweight youth. *Journal of Pediatric Psychology, 32*, 80–89.

Trout, J., & Graber, K. C. (2009). Perceptions of overweight students concerning their experience in physical education. *Journal of Teaching in Physical Education, 28*, 272–292.

Xiang, P., McBride, R., Bruene, A., & Liu, Y. (2007). Achievement goal patterns and their impact on fifth graders' motivation in physical education running programs. *Pediatric Exercise Science, 19*, 179–191.

Zeller, M. H., Reiter-Purtill, J., & Ramey, C. (2008). Negative peer perceptions of obese children in the classroom environment. *Obesity, 16*, 755–762.

5

STRATEGIES FOR INCLUSION IN PHYSICAL EDUCATION
APPLYING THE SOCIAL ECOLOGICAL CONSTRAINT MODEL

Guided by the Social Ecological Constraint Model, this chapter discusses practical strategies that physical education teachers can employ in their instruction methods to successfully include overweight or obese students in physical education classes. The first section discusses an urgent need to equip teachers with strategies to include overweight or obese students. The second section provides detailed information with regard to instructional strategies that physical education teachers can put in place to maximize overweight or obese students' motivation, engagement, and learning in physical education.

An Urgent Need: Equipping Physical Education Teachers with Strategies to Include Overweight or Obese Students

When compared to their peers with normal weight, obese or overweight students often display lower fitness and physical skills (Dumith et al., 2010; Okely, Booth, & Chey, 2004). They also suffer obesity-related health implications, experience psychosocial and emotional damage as a result of obesity bias, and are teased and excluded from physical education (Li & Ruka-vina, 2012b; Puhl & Latner, 2007; Trout & Graber, 2009). These obesity-associated negative attributes have presented serious challenges for physical education teachers to successfully include overweight or obese students in their group activities.

The National Association for Sport and Physical Education (2008) published the Standards for Initial Programs in Physical Education Teacher Education. Standard 3 states that physical education teachers shall plan and deliver developmentally appropriate learning experiences to meet the diverse needs of all students. To accomplish this standard, physical education teachers must provide individualized and differentiated instruction for diverse learners and create positive learning environments to maximize individual student learning.

Research, however, has shown that in-service and preservice physical education teachers are biased against overweight or obese students (Greenleaf & Weiller, 2005; Lynagh, Cliff, & Morgan, 2015; O'Brien, Hunter, & Banks, 2007). They generally have ill-conceived notions that overweight or obese students are inferior to their peers with normal weight. As a result, they have low expectations for overweight or obese students, and hold them less accountable for engagement, learning, and achieving success in their classes. Furthermore, in-service and preservice PE teachers are often less knowledgeable about how to effectively teach overweight or obese students by providing individualized and differentiated instruction as well as fostering inclusive, motivating, and safe learning environments (Li, Rukavina, Sutherland, Shen, & Kim, 2012).

The urgent need for inclusive strategies for teaching overweight or obese students in physical education is also reflected in a recent 2014 study, *Results from the School Health Policies and Practices* (CDC, 2015). The findings from this report indicated that 46% of teachers received professional development on how to promote active engagement and learning among overweight or obese students in physical education. Appropriately 22% of physical education teachers intend to attend a professional development on this topic (CDC, 2015). In summary, there is an urgent need to identify effective teaching strategies that physical education teachers can use to successfully include overweight or obese students in K–12 PE (Li & Rukavina, 2012a).

Strategies for Inclusion: Applying the Social Ecological Constraint Model

As discussed in Chapter 4, a variety of constraints at different levels of the Social Ecological Constraint Model can affect overweight or obese students' motivation, engagement, and learning in physical education. This section offers a variety of inclusive strategies for teaching overweight or obese students, with a goal of helping instructors successfully include overweight or obese students in physical education activities. These inclusive teaching strategies are derived from the proposed conceptual model of Social Ecological Constraint Model (Li & Rukavina, 2012a), the findings of a series of studies on inclusion of overweight or obese students in physical education (Doolittle, Rukavina, Li, Manson, & Beale, 2016; Rukavina, Doolittle, Li, Manson, & Beale, 2015), personal observations of K–12 physical education teaching, and personal dialogues with effective in-service teachers who have successfully worked with overweight or obese students in their teaching (Li, Li, Zhao, & Li, in press).

Teaching Strategies for Constraints at the Societal Level

Constraints at the societal level include legislation, policies, stigma/bias, and stereotypical beliefs in our society (Li & Rukavina, 2012a). Obesity bias/weight stigma is a significant societal constraint that negatively affects overweight or obese students' psychosocial and emotional well-being (Li & Rukavina, 2012b; Peterson, Puhl, & Luedicke, 2012; Puhl & Latner, 2007). In physical education, overweight or obese students experience obesity bias from not only their peers (Li & Rukavina, 2012b) but also their teachers (Greenleaf & Weiller, 2005; Lynagh et al., 2015; O'Brien et al., 2007). Physical education teachers should address obesity bias in their curriculum and develop policies to foster emotionally safe and inclusive learning environments and cultures, where overweight or obese students can be motivated to be engaged in learning. Physical education teachers can employ the following strategies to reduce or eliminate obesity bias and its negative effects.

• Critically analyze and reflect upon your own philosophical beliefs and instructional practices toward overweight or obese students. Physical education teachers should confront themselves on the biases that they hold against overweight or obese students and avoid using any teaching practices that can elicit the occurrence of bias and spotlight overweight or obese students in front of their peers (Li et al., in press).
Work with administrators and colleagues to develop a school-wide "no-bias" policy with clear and specific consequences and specific actions to report any bias when it occurs. This "no-bias" policy shall be implemented school-wide and have

a strong accountability system to ensure its effectiveness (Li et al., in press).

- Develop an instructional module on obesity bias and integrate it into regular physical education curriculum for all students. The module content can be the definition of obesity bias and its negative effects on overweight or obese students' psychosocial and emotional well-being, different types of obesity bias, environmental cues that can elicit obesity bias, and practical strategies to reduce or eliminate one's bias toward overweight or obese students. The purpose of this educational module is to raise students' awareness of their own stigmatized behaviors and obesity bias, evoke their sympathy toward overweight or obese students, and equip them with practical strategies to reduce and eliminate their obesity bias (Li et al., in press).

- Educate students that everyone has their own individual talents and empower each student with opportunities to showcase his or her talents in class. Physical education teachers should know each student's gifted area(s). It might be a sport, painting, drawing, singing, playing an instrument, writing, and so on. As a part of class routines, physical education teachers can provide opportunities for overweight or obese students to demonstrate their gifted areas. For example, if singing is an overweight or obese student's talent, a teacher can empower this student with an opportunity to sing the national anthem before playing a tournament (Li et al., in press).

Teaching Strategies for Constraints at the Community Level

The constraints at the community level include physical infrastructure and resources, safety, and social cultures (Li & Rukavina, 2012a). The availability of these physical infrastructure and resources such as parks, playgrounds, swimming pools, and walking and biking trails is critical for overweight or obese students to develop and maintain a healthy, physically active lifestyle. Limited or no access to these physical infrastructures and resources can significantly reduce physical activity levels that overweight or obese students can reach outside school (Li et al., in press). Neighborhood safety is another critical constraint that can greatly impact overweight or obese students' daily physical activity levels. Overweight or obese students who live in a dangerous neighborhood where gun shots and violence often occur on the streets will have very little or no chance to play sports with friends in their neighborhood. Very often, parents keep their children inside the house to be safe. Physical education teachers should have some knowledge of the constraints existing in the community, and then make best use of these physical infrastructures and resources to increase overweight or obese students' physical activity levels.

Teaching Strategies for Constraints at the School Level

Constraints at the school level consist of school culture, school programs, policies, physical resources, and social support by principals, classroom teachers, school counselors, and nurses (Li et al., in press). Physical education teachers should strategically collaborate with their administrators and colleagues to build an activity-friendly physical and social environment for overweight or obese students to be actively engaged in physical activities before, during, and after school. Some inclusive strategies that PE instructors can employ in their teaching are presented next:

- Foster a health-oriented school culture—eating healthy and being physically active. Physical education teachers should design their instructional curriculum to focus on being healthy, nurturing the body, and taking care of one's self rather than getting thin or looking like a body builder. This can be done by hosting school health fairs, using academic integration curriculum to teach physical education (collaborating with math and science teachers to integrate physical education content into their curriculum), and hosting family night sporting and health and wellness events.

- Students can gain numerous health benefits from physical activity. Physical activity can enhance muscle strength and bone density and increase mental function, life quality, self-confidence, and self-esteem, and decrease the risk of cardiovascular and chronic diseases such as obesity, heart disease, blood pressure, cancers, chronic diseases, depression, and anxiety (Physical Activity Guidelines Advisory Committee, 2008). Physical education teachers should advocate the health benefits of physical activity through a Comprehensive School-Wide Physical Activity Program (CSPAP). The CSPAP is a coordinated effort among all school personnel to provide opportunities for students to be physically active both in and out of school, with a goal to develop and maintain a physically active lifestyle and meet the nationally recommended at least 60 minutes of daily physical activity (CDC, 2013). Through the CSPAP, physical education teachers can gain more resources and supports from administrators and classroom colleagues to buy necessary equipment, incorporate new content into curriculum, and establish new programs, thus accommodating overweight or obese students' skill levels and needs (Li et al., in press).
- Physical activity is associated with better brain functions and higher levels of academic achievement among students (Erickson, Hillman, & Kramer, 2015). Research has shown

that an increased allocation of time to physical education had no negative effect on students' academic performance (Sallis et al., 1999). Therefore, physical education teachers should advocate the cognitive benefits of physical education and physical activity in their school to gain more resources and time allocation for physical education, recess, and before- and after-school programs (Li et al., in press).

- In an activity-friendly physical and social environment, overweight or obese students will have more opportunities to be physically active and gain new friends. Physical education teachers should create an activity-friendly physical and social environment through collaborations with principals and other school personnel. They can build an activity-friendly playground such as an area with interactive music combined with physical activities, and establish before- or after-school running clubs or lifetime fitness programs for overweight or obese students (Li et al., in press).

Teaching Strategies for Constraints at the Family Level

Parents are an important socializer who play a key role in affecting their children's motivation (Gonzalez-DeHass, Willems, & Holbein, 2005), academic performance (Senechal & LeFevre, 2002), and lifestyle behaviors such as exercising and maintaining healthier eating habits (Lindsay, Sussner, Kim, & Gortmaker, 2006). Parents' exercise knowledge, attitudes, and behaviors impact the development of lifestyle behaviors among their children (Kaplan, Liverman, & Kraak, 2005). They are a central part of national campaigns to reduce the epidemic of childhood obesity (Epstein, 1996; Lindsay et al., 2006). Constraints at the family level include parental attitudes and behaviors, home environment, parental educational background, parental social support, siblings' attitudes and behaviors, and parent–child interactions and relations. By recognizing the constraints at the family level, physical education teachers can strategically work with parents to help their overweight or obese student develop and maintain a healthy, physically active lifestyle. Some strategies that physical education teachers can use are presented next:

- Many parents of overweight or obese students lack scientific knowledge of obesity and its consequences, how to exercise, and nutrition. Physical education teachers should educate parents about the etiology of obesity and how to exercise correctly and eat healthy by sending weekly newsletters or brochures home to all students and their parents (Li et al., in press). This scientific information can raise parents' awareness of obesity and enable them to make informed decisions to improve their children's overall health and well-being. Other information can be included in the weekly newsletter or brochure: weight-related teasing and its negative effect on overweight or obese children's psychosocial and emotional well-being, community resources and programs for exercises and nutrition, and how to motivate children to exercise and eat healthy (Li et al., in press).

- Physical education teachers should work with parents of overweight or obese students to develop an exercise and nutrition plan to help their child to develop and maintain a healthy, physically active lifestyle (Li et al., in press).

- Overweight or obese students are often teased in physical education (Li & Rukavina, 2012b). PE teachers and school counselors can collaborate to provide parents with a list of adaptive coping strategies, thus helping their overweight or obese children to effectively handle teasing and reduce the negative consequences of teasing. These strategies include ignoring it, walking away, reporting teasing to teachers or the front office, and telling the teaser how you feel (Li et al., in press).

Teaching Strategies for Constraints at the Individual and Instructional Settings Levels

As discussed in Chapter 4, numerous constraints at the individual level and the instructional level can affect the inclusion of overweight or obese students. Since constraints at the individual and instructional settings levels are closely related to each other, we will discuss these teaching strategies for both levels together in this section.

Adopt a "the Same but Different" Inclusive Teaching Philosophy (Doolittle et al., 2016)

Physical education teachers should treat all students the same and also provide developmentally appropriate instruction and practices to address the needs of overweight or obese students. They should expect all students to perform the activities to the best of their ability. Physical education teachers should also recognize that some overweight or obese students may be in a normal stage of rapid growth and development, and being overweight may be a temporary condition. Physical education teachers can slightly modify the regular tasks to easily accommodate the majority of overweight students into regular class activities. Treating overweight or obese students dramatically differently would segregate them from the rest of the class (Doolittle et al., 2016). For the most challenging overweight or obese students who are unmotivated and do not want to participate in physical education, instructors should first build a caring relationship with them and then strategically select curricular content and activities to address the needs and growth of this subgroup of overweight or obese students.

Let Students Change Clothes in a Private Location
(Li et al., in press)

Many overweight or obese students are self-conscious of their body weight and do not feel comfortable changing in front of their peers. Teasing often occurs in the locker room where overweight or obese students' peers can easily see their body features (Li & Rukavina, 2012b). Therefore, physical education teachers should have overweight students changing their clothes in an area of the locker room without any kids back there. If overweight or obese students still feel uncomfortable, instructors can have them change their clothes in the bathroom, in the male or female teacher's office, or in stalls (a booth, cubicle, or stand) rather than in the locker room (Li et al., in press).

Modify Unit Goals and Content to Accommodate
Overweight Students' Skill Levels and Abilities
(Li et al., in press)

Physical education teachers should set individualized goals for overweight or obese students and select content that is developmentally appropriate for them to learn in physical education (Li et al., in press). They can let an overweight or obese student set a goal of 10 sit-ups if he or she can only perform 6 sit-ups. Physical education teachers can integrate tai chi, yoga, and adventure or cooperative activities into their unit and content rather than solely focusing on sports.

Design Learning Tasks by Student Ability Levels

In physical education, students will have different levels of ability and skills in sports. To provide developmentally appropriate instruction and practices to address the needs and growths of diverse learners, physical education instructors should design learning tasks by student ability levels. For example, in basketball, students can play against others who have similar skill levels and abilities. This can increase overweight or obese students' engagement in physical education.

Teach All Students How to Set Specific,
Measurable, Attainable, Realistic, and Timely
(SMART) Goals

Goal setting can assist students by directing their attention to a specific target, mobilizing their effort relative to the task demands, and providing a reference point to evaluate their performance as well as a reason to persist in the activity over time (Locke & Latham, 1990, 2002). Physical education teachers should teach all students how to set SMART goals. This teaching module can include the definition of a goal (something that one wants to achieve or attain), why goals are important (motivate us to act, give us direction, and tell us how we are doing), and two different types of goals (long term versus short term). A long-term goal is the one that will take some time and effort to achieve. For example, to get an A in physical education class for the year is a long-term goal. A short-term goal is the smaller, more easily attainable goal that helps us reach our long-term goals. For example, running 20 minutes five days a week is a short-term goal. Physical education teachers can teach students how to set a SMART goal (Locke & Latham, 1990, 2002),

S Specific—tell *exactly* what you want to happen, **what** you are going to do, **why** it is important to you, and **how** you are going to do it.
M Measurable—be able to see your progress.
A Attainable—be within your reach.
R Realistic—doable for you.
T Timely—give a specific time frame.

After students master the skills to set a SMART goal, they should be taught how to track and monitor their goals and remove barriers or obstacles that prevent them from reaching their goals. If a goal is met, students need to stretch themselves and make it a little harder. If a goal is not met, students need to find out why and make changes. There are several things for consideration when goals are not met.

1. Is your goal attainable and realistic for you? If not, set a more attainable and realistic goal.
2. Are specific things getting in the way of you achieving your goal?
   a. Identify possible blocks that may keep you from reaching your goals.
   b. Identify things that can be done to avoid or lessen these obstacles or blocks and act on them.
   c. Who can you turn to for help?

Offer Choices for Every Student to Enhance Their Motivation (Li et al., in press)

Physical education teachers can empower students with choices to increase their motivation in physical education (Hellison & Walsh, 2002; Prusak & Darst, 2002; Prusak, Treasure, Darst, & Pangrazi, 2004; Standage, Duda, & Ntoumanis, 2005). They can offer different pieces of equipment, provide various tasks/skill difficulty levels, and allow options of various types of activities (Mosston & Ashworth, 2002). For example, during a warm-up activity, overweight or obese students can choose to keep their body up in a plank position for 15 seconds or get to where they can do 10 push-ups. If we can give overweight or obese students different choices and not point it out to them in front of the entire class, this can motivate them to be engaged in activities. You do not want to point it out as it can make overweight or obese students feel embarrassed in front of their peers. You can go up to an individual overweight or obese student and tell him or her about the choices in person. Motivation is what it is all about. As a teacher, if you are motivated and show that you're motivated to overweight or obese students, then they will become motivated as well. For example, a physical education teacher can congratulate an overweight or obese student for holding her or his body up for 15 seconds by going up to him or her and speaking privately.

Provide Positive Feedback, Not Using a Negative Word

Positive feedback can make students feel good about themselves, thus motivating them to be more engaged in physical education. Physical education teachers should use phrases like "Try this" or "This will work better if you do this" to encourage overweight or obese students, rather than saying "Don't do this" or "You can't do that." Providing positive feedback and appropriate instructions to overweight or obese students who are not very skilled will help them build confidence in their abilities and become more engaged in physical education.

Do Not Single Out Overweight Students and Do Not Put Them into Spotlights by Making Drastic Modifications for Them (Li et al., in press)

In general, physical education teachers will need to make task modifications to address the needs of overweight or obese students. Physical education teachers should be cautious as to the degree to which they make these task modifications as these changes can have unintended negative consequences. When physical education teachers make drastic modifications specifically for overweight or obese students, the other students in the class will recognize what is going on. In a sense, you are unintentionally bringing attention to overweight or obese students and attention to their body weight. For example, physical education teachers should not allow overweight or obese students to sit on the bleaches while their peers are running (Li et al., in press).

Keep All Students Busy; No Time for Watching Whether
Other Kids Achieve or Not
(Li et al., in press)

This strategy works best when teachers can effectively organize and manage their class activities. For example, when students are performing crunches, they will do this activity in partners at the same time in different stations. It is so organized that no one is able to watch anyone else to see if he or she is achieving more or less. No one feels like "Oh, I only did five crunches and everyone saw me" because everyone is busy. Physical education teachers can watch and see if students are doing crunches correctly and recording their data on the score sheet accurately.

Grade Students on Personal and Social Responsibility
in Addition to Skills and Game Performance
(Li et al., in press)

Higher levels of personal and social responsibility are associated with higher levels of motivation and better social behaviors among students (Hellison & Walsh, 2002; Li, Wright, Rukavina, & Pickering, 2008). In order to develop personal and social responsibility among students, physical education teachers can make personal and social responsibility part of their grading criteria. Students will be graded according to how they treat each other and how they act in the locker room and in the gym (Li et al., in press). This can make gym classes more sociable and emotionally safe for overweight or obese students, and classroom management will be easier.

Focus on Personal Improvement by Using Progress Report Cards

Research has shown that students are more likely to display adaptive motivational and behavioral responses in a learning climate where personal improvement and task mastery are emphasized as learning goals (Xiang, McBride, Bruene, & Liu, 2007). Using progress report cards can focus students on personal improvement and task mastery rather than social comparisons and superiority over their peers. This task-oriented learning environment can motivate overweight or obese students to be more engaged in learning in physical education. The first time implementing progress report cards can be a little tough as students may not respond to this task well. It will go much smoother later on when students get used to it.

Work with Overweight Students on Diets and Get Them Involved in Playing Sports

Physical education teachers should go the extra mile to help overweight or obese students develop and maintain a healthy, physically active lifestyle. Physical education teachers can invite overweight or obese students to eat breakfast and lunch with them every day and help students make good food choices. Teachers can also do workouts with students after school. This effort can also help physical education teachers to build good interpersonal rapport with overweight or obese students, thus motivating them to become more engaged in physical education.

Use Stations (Li et al., in press)

Overweight or obese students do not like to perform physical activities in front of their peers when they are being watched by everyone else. Especially when it comes to fitness testing and activities, overweight or obese students do not want to run with someone who is comparatively fast. Physical education teachers can use stations where students can work hard at what they are doing in small groups. There will be only a couple of students next to them who may also be struggling at completing their challenges (Li et al., in press). Using stations can help overweight or obese avoid being embarrassed in front of the entire class due to inferior skills and abilities in sports.

Pay More Attention to Overweight Students and Care for Them (Li et al., in press)

Research has shown that students are more likely to be engaged in learning in physical education classes when their teachers are willing to work with them and have a caring attitude toward them (Cothran & Ennis, 1999, 2000; Larson, 2006; Zhao, Li, Kim, Xie, & Li, in press). Physical education teachers can build a caring relationship with their students through making instructional task adaptations, building interpersonal rapport, and creating a positive motivational learning climate (Li, 2015; Li, Rukavina, & Foster, 2013). There are times when overweight students may be a little more challenging. However, overweight students can be motivated to be engaged in learning in physical education if teachers pay a little more attention and spend more time with them. A list of comprehensive teaching strategies are provided to help physical education teachers build a caring relationship with their students, as reflected in Tables 5.1, 5.2, and 5.3.

Table 5.1 Teaching Strategies for Instructional Task Adaptations

Teaching strategies	Teaching scenarios	Teachers' actions
1. Break complex skills down into small parts to help students learn them.	During the practice of skipping, students had little success at performing skipping.	Teachers first have students practice step-hop on one foot, and then practice step-hop on the other foot. Next, students will practice step-hop with both feet in alternation. Finally, students will practice skipping with arms swinging in opposition.
2. Remind students of important parts of a skill continuously throughout the lesson.	The ball falls behind the partner when students practice the moving and passing task.	Teachers can remind students to keep the ball one step in front of the person who receives the ball.
3. Modify the movement requirements to accommodate students' abilities and skills (Winnick, 2011).	A student cannot run well.	Teachers can let him or her ride on a scooter so that he or she can be at the same speed with other students.
	A student cannot perform a full push-up.	Teachers can let students perform a modified push-up.
4. Offer help if students do not understand how to do a task.	During the instruction and demonstration of chest passing, a student cannot understand how to pronate the wrist.	Teachers personally show how to pronate the wrist to that student as many times as needed.
5. Provide cues on how students can improve their skills or learning in class.	In a rectangle, students practice a passing and moving task.	Teachers circulate among students to provide cues such as keeping thumbs down, following through, and moving to the open corner after passing, etc.

(Continued)

Table 5.1 (Continued)

Teaching strategies	Teaching scenarios	Teachers' actions
6. Make tasks that challenge students.	Some students quickly master the first two tasks: passing and moving and moving and passing.	Teachers provide a more difficult task for students to do by adding a warm defender (no stealing) so that they can work on creating an open passing lane while performing the moving and passing task.
7. Make sure to provide feedback on how students can perform the learning tasks better.	In a rectangle, students practice a passing and moving task.	Teachers provide positive, specific feedback: "Emma, I like how you execute the chest passing skill. It will be a perfect play if you can move to the open corner right away after you pass the ball out to your teammate."

Source: Li, W. (2015). Strategies for creating a caring learning climate in physical education. *Journal of Physical Education, Recreation and Dance, 86*, 34–41. Copyrights Permission Granted.

Table 5.2 Teaching Strategies for Building Interpersonal Rapport

Teaching strategies	Teaching scenarios	Teachers' actions
1. Make yourself available, provide materials, or establish programs to address students' needs.	A student forgets to bring a pencil for a test.	Teachers have some pencils prepared for them ahead of time.

(*Continued*)

Table 5.2 (Continued)

Teaching strategies	Teaching scenarios	Teachers' actions
	Some students show interest in having an after-school running program.	Teachers work with the principal to establish an after-school running program and volunteer their time to be the instructor.
2. Make students feel that they are important.	A student keeps silent during group discussions.	Teachers step in to let him or her have a voice in the topic being discussed.
3. Be nice to students in class.	A student is off task.	Teachers nicely redirect him or her to focus on the task with a smile rather than yelling or using a commanding language.
4. Make students feel that they are special.	Today is Emma's birthday.	Teachers can post a "Happy Birthday" sign onto the wall. Have the entire class sing the happy birthday song. Give Emma a sticker that says "I AM SPECIAL."
5. Use students' names.	The teacher uses students for skill demonstration.	Teachers say, "Emma and Emily, would you please show us how to do a chest pass."
6. Try to make personal connections with students	A "big size" student is unmotivated in class.	Teachers can have a chat with the student about why he or she is unmotivated and implement changes in teaching to increase his or her involvement in class.

(*Continued*)

Table 5.2 (Continued)

Teaching strategies	Teaching scenarios	Teachers' actions
7. Express concerns with students' well-being.	A "big size" student is out of breath during activities or games.	Teachers have a private chat with the student on how to develop and maintain a healthy, physically active lifestyle, perhaps in the conference room at the main office, or refer the student to see the school nurse.
8. Accept students for who they are.	A Muslim girl wears a hijab. Her peers stare at her and ask why she is wearing this in PE.	PE teachers in collaboration with classroom teachers can have students share their cultures to promote mutual understanding of one another.
9. Be patient and understanding with students.	A student still cannot execute the skill correctly after numerous practice trials.	Teachers verbally tell that student with a soft and nice tone, "I understand you are struggling. This is the part that many students have a tough time with." Teachers can allow him or her to have more time to work on the skill by providing more support and feedback, or can give him or her an alternative task to work on.
10. Treat students fairly and with respect.	During their supervision of practice, teachers circulate among students to provide feedback.	Teachers distribute their attention equally to all students rather than spending more time with students with high skill levels.

(*Continued*)

Table 5.2 (Continued)

Teaching strategies	Teaching scenarios	Teachers' actions
11. Listen to students.	The teacher poses a question to solicit perspectives from students.	Teachers allow enough time for students to voice their perspectives. Do not interrupt students or wrap it up in a hurry.

Source: Li, W. (2015). Strategies for creating a caring learning climate in physical education. *Journal of Physical Education, Recreation and Dance, 86*, 34–41. Copyrights Permission Granted.

Table 5.3 Teaching Strategies for Creating a Motivational Learning Climate

Teaching strategies	Teaching scenarios	Teachers' actions
1. Make teamwork an important part of class.	For the basketball unit, students will be grouped into teams. Each student will have a role and associated responsibility such as team captain, equipment manager, score keeper, etc. They will practice the skills together and compete as a team.	Teachers assign students into teams with equity in terms of gender and skill levels. Team members will work together to assign a role to each team member. Teachers will then teach the responsibilities of each of the team roles to students and ensure that students can fulfill their individual responsibilities.
2. Ask all of the students to try their best to improve their own performance in class.	Students practice the passing and moving in a rectangle.	Teachers instruct students to put forth their best effort for self-improvement, not focusing on how well they perform compared to their peers.

(*Continued*)

Table 5.3 (Continued)

Teaching strategies	Teaching scenarios	Teachers' actions
3. Empower students with choices and leaderships in learning.	At the beginning of the semester, teachers let students determine an activity or a sport for the last unit at their own choice.	In the first lesson of the semester, teachers allocate 8 minutes for students to discuss what activity or sport they want to do during the last unit and then select the top three activities or sports, put them on a ballot, and allow students to vote.
	At the start of a lesson, students perform warm-up and cool-down activities.	Teachers assign students to lead the warm-up and cool-down activities.
4. Provide opportunities for students to succeed in class, thus increasing their perceptions of competence.	During supervision, students have great difficulty in executing the moving and passing task from midcourt to the baseline.	Teachers have students practice the task in slow motion. When students can complete this modified task successfully, teachers move them back to the original task at a normal speed.
5. Emphasize the efficacy of effort, which is important to success in learning.	At the start of practicing the moving and passing task, students have some difficulty in performing the skill.	Teachers tell students that the more they practice, the better they will be at performing the skill. Ask them not to give up and tell them that hard work will pay off later.
6. Do not "put students on the spot" in front of peers.	During the fitness unit, students are performing push-ups and the number of push-ups	Teachers ask students to self-count how many push-ups they do and record the number on a

(*Continued*)

Table 5.3 (Continued)

Teaching strategies	Teaching scenarios	Teachers' actions
	will be counted and recorded.	piece of paper and give it back to the teachers, rather than having students count out loud and verbally report the number to teachers. This will avoid putting weak or "big size" students on the spot in front of peers.
7. Encourage and support students.	During the practice of the moving and passing task from midcourt to the baseline, students demonstrate a 65% successful rate at performing the task.	Teachers encourage them to keep trying and support them with feedback and cues to help them improve the skill.
8. Encourage students to set goals for themselves.	During the fitness unit, students are working on running a mile.	Teachers have students record how long it took them to finish a mile that day, and then work with them to set individualized goals for running a mile for the next lesson.
9. Make students feel safe in class.	Teachers provide instructions and demonstrations of soccer kicking skills.	Teachers remind students of safety and tell them if the ball goes out to other students' practice station, make sure to stop first and then ask peers to stop for them to retrieve the soccer ball.

(*Continued*)

Table 5.3 (Continued)

Teaching strategies	Teaching scenarios	Teachers' actions
10. Make students feel welcomed and comfortable every day.	Teachers present instructions and communicate to their students during lessons.	Teachers smile and use an enthusiastic, encouraging tone.
11. Motivate students to participate more in class.	During the team practice of the passing and moving task in a rectangle, one team captain quickly gets his or her team involved in practice. One teammate does not move after passing. The captain reminds his or her teammate to move after passing in an encouraging tone.	Teachers reward the team with a good behavior point by saying "I really like how quickly team A gets into practice and how the captain helps her teammate to learn the task. Team A will earn 2 points."
12. Set high expectations for students in class to push students to work harder in class.	Students practice basketball shooting for accuracy.	Teachers work with students to set individual goals regarding how many shots they want to make and then instruct students to practice hard to achieve their goals. Upon accomplishing their individual goals, students can move on to next task.
13. Make students feel they are being respected in class.	During practice, a student yells at his or her peer.	Teachers walk to that student and remind him or her of the need to respect others. During reflections at the end of the lesson, teachers debrief on

Table 5.3 (Continued)

Teaching strategies	Teaching scenarios	Teachers' actions
		why we should respect others and how to respect others in their classes and beyond their classes.
14. Encourage students to care for or help each other.	A first grade student's shoelace is loose.	Teachers can let peers who can tie a shoelace help that student tie the shoelace.
	During practice, a student has difficulty performing a chest pass, showing palms down following the passing.	Teachers find someone on the student's team who can correctly perform a chest pass and have that person work with him or her to correct the error (physically showing the performance again or giving verbal reminder of palms out).

Source: Li, W. (2015). Strategies for creating a caring learning climate in physical education. *Journal of Physical Education, Recreation and Dance, 86,* 34–41. Copyrights Permission Granted.

Empower Overweight Students with Leadership Opportunities

Physical education teachers can find out what overweight or obese students can do or are good at. They can use overweight students to demonstrate the skills or positions that they are good at. For example, in volleyball, a teacher can empower overweight or obese students with an opportunity to lead the class by asking them to demonstrate the positions.

Use the Fitnessgram PACER Test Rather Than a Mile Run

Physical education teachers should avoid using half a mile or a mile run to test students' cardiovascular capacity since overweight or obese students are always the last to complete the test. All the athletic students would be impatiently waiting for the obese or overweight student to finish. As a result, overweight or obese students would feel terrible. The beauty of Fitnessgram PACER test is that students who are more athletic are the ones who go at the end.

Instill Scientific Knowledge and Principles on Exercise and Eating

Many overweight or obese students and their parents lack scientific knowledge about principles of exercises and eating healthier meals. One parent of an overweight or obese student reported that her son walks one mile with her every evening. This parent could not understand why her son did not lose any body weight. Thus, it is critical for physical education teachers to equip overweight students and their parents with scientific knowledge and principles on exercise and eating habits. This knowledge package can include causes of obesity, an energy balance approach for weight loss, selection of exercises, how to eat healthy, how to design a scientifically sound workout, how to monitor eating and exercise, how to assess personal progress in exercises and eating, goal setting and motivation.

Create Intramural Programs and Organize and Sponsor Student Clubs and Structured Before- and After-School Programs for Students and Their Family

Social and physical support mechanisms play a large role in determining children's physical activity levels (Sallis & Owen

1999). Physically active teachers provide students with more physical fitness activities and allocate more time promoting physical fitness in their lessons (McKenzie, LaMaster, Sallis, & Marshall, 1999). Physically active parents (Trost et al., 2003) are linked with active children. Physical education teachers should work with school personnel and parents to create intramural programs and other programs for students who cannot make interscholastic sport teams to be physically active.

These intramural programs and clubs can focus on lifetime recreational sports and physical activities and nutrition and target other healthy lifestyle behaviors. They can address these marginalized students' physical activity needs. Very often, overweight or obese students are from low socioeconomic families. Parents may work two different jobs and do not have time to cook a proper meal for their children or play sports with them. Intramural programs provide social and physical support mechanisms that can increase opportunities for overweight or obese students to develop a healthy, physically active lifestyle. For example, a physical education teacher shared that she organizes a morning running club to all third through fifth graders on a first come, first serve basis each day. She cuts the number of participants off at 15 for supervision reasons. She also makes special exceptions for overweight/obese students who will always come to run. According to her, no one complains about it not being "fair." In addition, physical education teachers can collaborate with school nurses to offer an after-school health program for overweight or obese students and their parents. The program can be 12 two-hour sessions comprised of a one-hour lecture on nutrition and one-hour of activities and games. The nutrition talks give students some empowerment to choose the right kind of food to eat so that they can make wise decisions. The activities and games help overweight or obese students realize that playing games can be fun and at the same time keep them healthy.

Implement a Grading System That Includes Motor Skills,
Effort, Improvement, and Social Skills

Physical education teachers should use a grading system that can include each of these four components—motor skills, effort, improvement, and social skills. Each of these components can account for 25% of the grading rubric. If some students get dressed, show up, and actively participate in learning in physical education, they should be rewarded for their effort and participation. Even if these students do poorly on motor skills, they can still make it up in the other three categories by putting effort into improving their skills and being a good citizen in class. This inclusive grading system can motivate overweight or obese students to be more engaged in learning in physical education.

Change Game Rules for Better Inclusion
(Li et al., in press)

Physical education teachers can modify the game rules to promote better engagement among overweight or obese students. For example, in a soccer game, instructors can modify the game rules by not allowing a goalie. This will prevent any team from assigning overweight or obese students as a goalie, thus providing more opportunities for them to be more physically active during the soccer game (Li et al., in press).

Use an Alternative Instructional/Curricular Models
Rather Than Traditional Curriculum to Teach
Lifetime Skills and Personal and Social Growth
(Li et al., in press)

Traditionally, physical education curriculum has mainly focused on competitive sports. This has disadvantaged and marginalized overweight or obese students in terms of opportunities to be physically active in physical education. Overweight or obese students are often excluded from participating in sports as a result of not being selected by teams (Li & Rukavina, 2012b). To provide equitable opportunities for overweight or obese students to be physically active in physical education for better inclusion, instructors can focus on teaching lifetime skills and personal and social growth by using different curricula models. These curricular models include cooperative learning (Dyson & Casey, 2012), adventure education (Rohnke, 2009), teaching for personal and social responsibility (Hellison, 2011), and sport education (Siedentop, Hastie, & van der Mars, 2011).

Use Creative Managerial and Organization Strategies to Include Overweight Students (Li et al., in press)

Many creative managerial and organization strategies can be used for better inclusion of overweight or obese students. One of these strategies is to use a "buddy" system. Physical education teachers can partner an overweight or obese student with a nice "buddy," who has a normal weight and can provide social support for this overweight or obese student. This can help overweight or obese students feel more comfortable engaging in physical education activities, and can buffer them from the negative interactions with biased peers.

Do a Timed Run Rather Than a Mile Walk or Run (Li et al., in press)

Very often, overweight or obese students are the last to finish a mile walk or run. They have to finish the last couple of laps while the rest of the class stands around watching them. This makes overweight or obese students feel inadequate, embarrassed, and hurt especially when their peers make some negative comments about their effort or performance. To avoid putting overweight or obese students in this awkward situation, physical education teachers can have the class run for a certain number of minutes. They can assign a grade based on the time when they stop walking or running. Doing it this way will ensure that all students are at the same level, no one is isolated, and overweight or obese students will not feel embarrassed about themselves (Li et al., in press).

Create a Safe Environment for All Students

A safe environment is key to students' active engagement in physical education classes. When students feel safe, they are more likely to be engaged in learning. Thus, physical education teachers should establish a safe environment from the beginning of the school year by setting clear class expectations, rules, and routines. When these class expectations, rules, and routines are drilled into children, in a positive and fun way, of course, then the environment is more likely to be safe for all students, regardless of weight or other insecurity issues. Physical education teachers can also do many cooperative team activities for a couple weeks to build teamwork and cooperation among students right from the beginning. In addition, physical education teachers can do "appreciations" at the end of each lesson. For example, physical education teachers can show appreciation if a student takes time to help his or her teammate who is confused about the learning task, or if a student puts forth a great deal of effort that day.

Educate All Students That Everyone Has Their Own Gifted Areas

Students should be aware that everyone has different talents and is gifted in different areas. Some students are good at sports, while others are good at math, science, reading, arts, or music. Even within sports, some students are good at running, while others are good at basketball, gymnastics, or other sports. Educating students about this will help build a basic understanding and appreciation of one another, which will help boost all students' confidence by recognizing their gifted areas and will motivate students to improve their areas of weakness.

Teach Overweight Students Social Skills or Coping Strategies to Deal with Negative Social Interactions or Teasing (Doolittle et al., 2016)

Social interactions affect overweight or obese students' ability to participate successfully with their peers in physical education (Doolittle et al., 2016). Research has demonstrated that the majority of overweight or obese students are teased in physical education classes (Li & Rukavina, 2012b), and they have adopted numerous maladaptive coping strategies to deal with weight-related teasing and its negative effects on their well-being (Li, Rukavina, & Wright, 2012). In Chapter 4, a list of adaptive coping strategies was provided. It is suggested that physical education instructors teach these coping strategies to overweight or obese students so that they are well equipped to cope against weight-related teasing and its negative effects.

Summary

In this chapter, we shared numerous teaching strategies guided by the Social Ecological Constraints Model (Li & Rukavina, 2012a) to successfully include overweight or obese students in physical education. Including overweight or obese students in physical education classes successfully is a challenge for teachers given that there are so many constraints existing at multiple levels of an ecology, such as beliefs, attitudes, motivation, bias, lack of space, resources, scheduling, and policy restrictions. Some overweight or obese students may be more challenging than others. To effectively include overweight or obese students in physical education, a comprehensive, school-wide approach with multiple strategies should be used to manipulate the modifiable constraints at all five levels (Li et al., in press). Physical education teachers should first build a trusting, caring relationship with overweight or obese students through simple encouragement phrases, private conversations, an open-door policy, and other teaching methods and then intervene further by seeking their input on curricular content and program requirements and tackling poor attitudes and behaviors of peers demonstrated in class (Doolittle et al., 2016). Physical education teachers very often need to go out of their ways to help these at-risk vulnerable students. When physical education teachers experience difficulty or even failure, they should recognize that they are not alone in solving these issues. Physical education teachers can seek information from professional colleagues at school or collaborate with parents and other professionals to develop strategies to better engage overweight or obese students in learning in class (Doolittle et al., 2016).

As Doolittle et al. (2016) pointed out, there are limits to what physical education teachers can do to help out overweight or obese students, and the issue of overweight or obesity is a very "touchy subject" in schools. Therefore, physical education instructors should approach this issue carefully and with sensitivity. Some parents of overweight or obese students may not perceive being overweight as an issue, and they may be resistant to perceived criticism and reject any offerings of adapted and remedial programs (Doolittle et al., 2016). However, this should not prevent physical education teachers from working with overweight or obese students to improve their overall health, well-being, and quality of life. Quite often, children are able to teach their parents healthy behavioral activities, thus becoming agents of change for their family and community.

This chapter provided a number of inclusive strategies for physical education teachers to use for better inclusion of overweight or obese students. Physical education teachers should treat these strategies as a starting point, and then use the Social Ecological Constraint Model as a conceptual guide to develop more creative, innovative inclusive strategies to increase overweight or obese students' engagement and learning in physical education (Li et al., in press). Physical education teachers should also be mindful that individual personalities and traits and school contexts can affect the degree of effectiveness of these inclusive strategies. Therefore, when implementing these inclusive strategies, physical education teachers should be flexible and open-minded (Li et al., in press). If one strategy does not work, modify it or move on to another strategy. Through trial and error, physical education teachers can develop a repertoire of inclusive strategies that can work better for their students.

References

Centers for Disease Control and Prevention. (2013). *Comprehensive school physical activity programs: A guide for schools.* Atlanta, GA: U.S. Department of Health and Human Services.

Centers for Disease Control and Prevention. (2015). Results from the school health policies and practices study 2014. Atlanta, GA: U.S. Department of Health and Human Services. Available at: http://www.cdc.gov/healthy youth/data/shpps/pdf/shpps-508-final_101315.pdf

Cothran, D. J., & Ennis, C. D. (1999). Alone in a crowd: Meeting students' needs for relevance and connection in urban high school physical education. *Journal of Teaching in Physical Education, 18*, 234–247.

Cothran, D. J., & Ennis, C. D. (2000). Building bridges to student engagement: Communicating respect and care for students in urban high schools. *Journal of Research & Development in Education, 33*, 106–117.

Doolittle, S., Rukavina, P. B., Li, W., Manson, M., & Beale, A. (2016). Middle school physical education teachers' perspectives on overweight students. *Journal of Teaching in Physical Education, 35*, 127–137.

Dumith, S. C., Ramires, W., Souza, M. A., Moraes, D. S., Petry, F. G., Oliveira, E. S., . . . Hallal P. C. (2010). Overweight/obesity and physical fitness among children and adolescents. *Journal of Physical Activity and Health, 7,* 641–648.

Dyson, B., & Casey, A. (Eds.) (2012). *Cooperative learning in physical education: A research based approach.* London, UK: Routledge.

Epstein, L. (1996). Family based behavioral intervention for obese children. *International Journal of Obesity and Related Metabolic Disorders, 20*(1), s14–s21.

Erickson, K. I., Hillman, C. H., & Kramer, A. F. (2015). Physical activity, brain, and cognition. *Current Opinion in Behavioral Sciences, 4,* 27–32.

Gonzalez-Dehass, A. R., Willems, P. P., & Holbein, M. F. D. (2005). Examining the relationship between parental involvement and student motivation. *Educational Psychology Review, 17,* 99–123.

Greenleaf, C., & Weiller, K. (2005). Perceptions of youth obesity among physical educators. *Social Psychology of Education, 8,* 407–423.

Hellison, D. (2011). *Teaching for personal and social responsibility through physical activity* (3rd ed.). Champaign, IL: Human Kinetics.

Hellison, D., & Walsh, D. (2002). Responsibility-based youth programs evaluation: Investigating the investigations. *Quest, 54,* 292–307.

Kaplan, J. P., Liverman, C. T., & Kraak, V. I. (2005). *Preventing childhood obesity: Health in the balance.* Washington, DC: The National Academies Press.

Larson, A. (2006). Student perception of caring teaching in physical education. *Sport, Education, and Society, 11,* 337–352.

Li, H., Li, W., Zhao, Q., & Li, M. (in press). Including overweight or obese students in physical education: An urgent need and effective teaching strategies. *Journal of Physical Education, Recreation and Dance.*

Li, W. (2015). Strategies for creating a caring learning climate in physical education. *Journal of Physical Education, Recreation and Dance, 86,* 34–41.

Li, W., & Rukavina, P. (2012a). Including overweight or obese students in physical education: A social ecological constraint model. *Research Quarterly for Exercise and Sports, 83,* 570–578.

Li, W., & Rukavina, P. (2012b). The nature, occurring contexts, and psychological implications of weight-related teasing in urban physical education programs. *Research Quarterly for Exercise and Sport, 83,* 308–317.

Li, W., Rukavina, P., & Foster, C. (2013). Overweight or obese students' perceptions of caring in urban physical education programs. *Journal of Sport Behavior, 32,* 189–208.

Li, W., Rukavina, P., Sutherland, S., Shen, B., & Kim, I. (2012). Physical education in the eyes of overweight or obese adolescents' parents. *Journal of Sport Behavior, 35,* 204–222.

Li, W., Rukavina, P., & Wright, P. M. (2012). Coping against weight-related teasing among overweight or obese adolescents in urban physical education. *Journal of Teaching in Physical Education, 31,* 182–199.

Li, W., Wright, P. M., Rukavina, P., & Pickering, M. (2008). Measuring students' perceptions of personal and social responsibility and its relationship to intrinsic motivation in urban physical education. *Journal of Teaching in Physical Education, 27*, 167–178.

Lindsay, A. C., Sussner, K. M., Kim, J., & Gortmaker, S. (2006). The role of parents in preventing childhood obesity. *The Future of Children, 16*, 169–186.

Locke, E. A., & Latham, G. P. (1990). *A theory of goal setting and task performance.* Englewood Cliffs, NJ: Prentice-Hall.

Locke, E. A., & Latham, G. P. (2002). Building a practically useful theory of goal setting and task motivation: A 35-year odyssey. *American Psychologist, 57*, 705–717.

Lynagh, M., Cliff, K., & Morgan, P. J. (2015). Attitudes and beliefs of nonspecialist and specialist trainee health and physical education teachers toward obese children: Evidence for "anti-fat" bias. *Journal of School Health, 85*, 595–603.

McKenzie, T. L., LaMaster, K. J., Sallis, J. F., & Marshall, S. J. (1999). Classroom teachers' leisure time physical activity and their conduct of physical education. *Journal of Teaching in Physical Education, 19*, 125–131.

Mosston, M., & Ashworth, S. (2002). *Teaching physical education* (5th ed.). San Francisco, CA: Benjamin Cummins.

National Association for Sport and Physical Education. (2008). *National standards for beginning physical education teachers.* Reston, VA: Author.

O'Brien, K. S., Hunter, J. A., & Banks, M. (2007). Implicit anti-fat bias in physical educators: Physical attributes, ideology and socialization. *International Journal of Obesity, 31*, 308–314.

Okely, A. D., Booth, M. L., & Chey, T. (2004). Relationships between body composition and fundamental movement skills among children and adolescents. *Research Quarterly for Exercise and Sport, 75*, 238–247.

Peterson, J. L., Puhl, R. M., & Luedicke, J. (2012). An experimental assessment of physical educators' expectations and attitudes: The importance of student weight and gender. *Journal of School Health, 82*(9), 432–440. doi: 10.1111/j1746-1561.2012.00719

Physical Activity Guidelines Advisory Committee. (2008). *Physical activity guidelines advisory committee report.* Washington, DC: U.S. Department of Health and Human Services.

Prusak, K. A., & Darst, P. W. (2002). Effects of types of walking activities on actual choices by adolescent female physical education students. *Journal of Teaching in Physical Education, 21*, 230–241.

Prusak, K. A., Treasure, D. C., Darst, P. W., & Pangrazi, R. P. (2004). The effects of choice on the motivation of adolescent girls in physical education. *Journal of Teaching in Physical Education, 23*, 19–29.

Puhl, R., & Latner, J. D. (2007). Stigma, obesity, and the health of the nation's children. *Psychological Bulletin, 133*, 557–580.

Rohnke, K. (2009). *Silver bullets: A revised guide to initiative problems, adventure games and trust activities* (2nd ed.). Beverly, MA: Project Adventure, Inc.

Rukavina, P. B., Doolitttle, S., Li, W., Manson, M., & Beale, A. (2015). Middle school teachers' strategies for including overweight students in skill and fitness instruction. *Journal of Teaching in Physical Education, 34*, 93–118. doi: 10.1123/jtpe.2013–0152

Sallis, J. F., McKenzie, T. L., Kolody, B., Lewis, M., Marshall, S., & Rosengard, P. (1999). Effects of health-related physical education on academic achievement: Project SPARK. *Research Quarterly for Exercise and Sport, 70*, 127–134.

Sallis, J. F., & Owen, N. (1999). *Physical activity and behavioral medicine.* Thousand Oaks, CA: Sage Publications.

Senechal, M., & LeFevre, J. (2002). Parental involvement in the development of children's reading skill: A five-year longitudinal study. *Child Development, 73*, 445–460.

Siedentop, D., Hastie, P., & van der Mars, H. (2011). *Complete guide to sport education* (3rd ed.). Champaign, IL: Human Kinetics.

Standage, M., Duda, J. L., & Ntoumanis, N. (2005). A test of self-determination theory in school physical education. *British Journal of Educational Psychology, 75*, 411–433.

Trost, S., Sallis, J., Russell, P., Freedson, P., Taylor, W., & Dowda, M. (2003). Evaluating a model of parental influence on youth physical activity. *American Journal of Preventive Medicine, 25*(4), 277–282.

Trout, J., & Graber, K. C. (2009). Perceptions of overweight students concerning their experience in physical education. *Journal of Teaching in Physical Education, 28*, 272–292.

Winnick, J. (2011). *Adapted physical education and sport (5th ed.).* Champaign, IL: Human Kinetics.

Xiang, P., McBride, R., Bruene, A., & Liu, Y. (2007). Achievement goal patterns and their impact on fifth graders' motivation in physical education running programs. *Pediatric Exercise Science, 19*, 179–191.

Zhao, Q., Li, W., Kim, J., Xie, X., & Li, Y. (in press). Measuring perceptions of teachers' caring behaviors and its relationship to motivational responses in physical education among middle school students. *Physical Educator.*

INDEX

run/walk 109–10; working on
  diet 95
instructional task adaptations 97–8
interventions for overweight
  students: allowing privacy when
  changing 90; before- and after-
  school sports programs 106–7;
  building rapport 98–100, 112;
  differentiated instruction 74,
  82; do not single out overweight
  students 93–4; involving
  overweight students in sports
  95; paying attention 96; positive
  feedback 93; teaching social
  skills and coping strategies 111;
  working on diet 95; *see also*
  coping strategies for obesity bias
intramural programs 106–7

leadership opportunities 105
learning environment, safe 110
learning tasks, designed to match
  ability levels 90–1
lifestyle behaviors, causing obesity
  5–6
lifetime skills 108–9
losing weight 56; *see also* diet

managerial strategies, creative 109
medical conditions causing obesity 5
mile run/walk 106, 109–10
motivation 73, 92–3, 101–5
motor skills 108

National Association for Sport and
  Physical Education 81
normal (healthy) weight BMI 2

obese BMI 2
obese students *see* overweight
  students
obesity: defined 1–2; emotional
  consequences of 68, 81; etiology
  of 4–6, 36; financial costs of 8,

11; physiological consequences
  of 6–7, 11, 68; prevalence of 4,
  11; psychosocial consequences
  of 7, 11, 68, 81; stigmatization of
  16–17, 68; *see also* obesity bias
obesity bias: conceptual
  frameworks for reduction
  26–32; consequences of 22–6;
  as constraint 76; defined 17–18;
  and empathy 26, 29–30, 36;
  locations occurring 22; in
  physical education classes 18–19,
  81; in physical education teachers
  33–5, 83; societal 72; strategies
  for physical education teachers
  32–3; *see also* coping strategies for
  obesity bias
organization strategies, creative 109
overweight BMI 2
overweight students: avoid singling
  out 93–4; consequences of
  obesity bias 24–5; empowerment
  of 105; exclusion of 20, 22, 69,
  76; individual gifts and abilities
  of 37, 84, 110; involvement in
  sports 95; paying attention to 96;
  strategies for inclusion 81–2; *see
  also* coping strategies for obesity
  bias; interventions for overweight
  students

parental support 61–5, 87–9; *see
  also* family involvement
peer victimization 7; *see also*
  bullying; teasing
perceived social consensus model
  31–2
personal growth 108–9
personal improvement 95, 108
perspective taking 29–30
physical activity: cognitive and
  academic benefits 10–11, 86–7;
  physical and psychosocial benefits
  of 8–9, 11

teasing: coping strategies for 111;
  fights resulting from 21; ignoring/
  disengaging 48–9; and parental
  support 61–5; reinforced by
  teacher 21–2; school-wide
  policy against 37–8; strategies
  for responding to 52, 57–9;
  stress resulting from 52; teacher
response to 35; weight-related 3,
  7, 17–18, 20, 24, 29, 32, 36, 45, 47,
  50–6, 60–3, 69, 81, 88–90
timed runs 106, 109–10

underweight BMI 2

weight stigma *see* obesity bias